BASEBALL'S SIXTH TOOL

PLAYING THE MENTAL GAME
TO GET THE COMPETITIVE EDGE

MARK GOLA

Mc Graw Hill

New York   Chicago   San Francisco   Lisbon   London   Madrid   Mexico City
Milan   New Delhi   San Juan   Seoul   Singapore   Sydney   Toronto

Library of Congress Cataloging-in-Publication Data

Gola, Mark.
    Baseball's sixth tool : playing the mental game to get the competitive edge /
Mark Gola.
        p.   cm.
    Includes index.
    ISBN 13: 978-0-07-154515-0 (alk. paper)
    ISBN 10: 0-07-154515-8 (alk. paper)
    1. Baseball—Psychological aspects.   I. Title.

GV867.6.G65   2008
796.35701'9—dc22   2007035633

1 2 3 4 5 6 7 8 9 10 11 12 13 14 15 16 17 18 19 DOC/DOC 0 9 8

ISBN 978-0-07-154515-0
MHID   0-07-154515-8

Interior photographs by Michael Plunkett

McGraw-Hill books are available at special quantity discounts to use as premiums and sales promotions or for use in corporate training programs. To contact a representative, please visit the Contact Us pages at www.mhprofessional.com.

This book is printed on acid-free paper.

To my collegiate baseball teammates and coaches at Rider (1991–1994). Playing baseball with you guys was priceless. Thanks for the friendships and memories.

Butch Bellenger, Brian Berhard, Scott Bloszinski, Rich Brady, Jerry Brendle, Shawn Brown, Joe Cerasi, John Crane, Mike D'Andrea, John Davis, Chris Dearth, Jeff Dillman, Joe Dorety, Joe Doto, Mel Edwards, Jeff Fennelli, Brian Farrell, Shaun Figueroa, Ernie Fisher, Bob Furlong, Eric Garnett, Tony Garrison, Joe Gmitter, Rob Gontkosky, Jim Gordon, John Gray, Pat Hallanan, Chris Hart, John Haydu, Brian Humphrey, Bernard Hunt, Jim Hutchinson, Tom Kerr, Jason Klonis, Jason Koehler, Rich Kraemer, Steve Kraemer, Kevin Lazarski, Phil Ledesma, John Long, Dan Mahony, John Malosh, Levi Miskolczi, Johnny Montes, Willie Montes, Craig Pacelli, Anthony Rawa, Mike Reenock, Joe Ruffino, Jaime Scheck, Jim Schlotter, Jason Steinert, Rudy Siegel, Rob Van Zile, Scott Wayda, Dan Wilson, Mike Zuppe.

Coaches: Sonny Pittaro, Jeff Plunkett, Rick Freeman

Sports Information Director: Bud Focht

Contents

Foreword by Mike Hazen, Director
of Player Development, Boston Red Sox   vii

Preface   ix

Acknowledgments   xiii

1 Character   1

2 Baserunning   29

3 Defense   63

4 Pitching   93

5 Hitting   121

Index   149

Foreword

Every professional baseball player has talent. However one calculates their tools, professional players can consistently reproduce their physical skills on the field, whether they run fast, throw hard, spin a breaking ball, or hit with power. These are skills most players are born with and strive every day to embellish in batting practice, fielding practice, or bullpen sessions. How these physical tools develop usually garners the majority of focus in evaluating prospects.

Professional baseball players have the opportunity during the season to practice their skills every day for nearly six months, and they continue to work out during the off-season. There is no shortage of game or practice repetition, and players who are committed to their careers will have an edge in maximizing their physical potential. So if all professional baseball players have talent and ample opportunities to work on their physical skills, what separates one player from the next? In order to realize the dream of getting to the major leagues, these players must develop skills beyond their physical tools.

Certainly there are players with rare abilities that separate them from the pack—Josh Beckett, Alex Rodriguez, Jose Reyes, and Vladimir Guerrero, to name a few. A large majority of players, however, don't have exceptional tools in every facet of the game. Pitchers who do not throw 95 miles per hour consistently have to develop a "feel" to pitch; throwing strikes with multiple pitches and knowing how to attack their opposition will give them an edge. Hitters who do not possess the ability to hit .330 with power have to be adept at taking the extra base or maximizing their versatility on defense by having the knowledge to play multiple positions.

Boston Red Sox second baseman Dustin Pedroia is an excellent example of a player who learned to play above his raw physical skills. Dustin possesses exceptional baseball intelligence, instincts, and defensive versatility along with a tireless work ethic and passion for the game. These skills have enabled him to become one of the best second basemen in baseball.

Much like raw physical tools, versatility, aggressiveness, intelligence, and character are tremendous assets for a baseball player. Unlike those physical tools, these sixth-tool skills are within the complete control of the player. Physical skills can be improved through hard work, but every player has his individual ceiling. Sixth-tool skills are boundless and can be acquired by any player who is passionate and attentive.

Baseball's Sixth Tool presents new and exciting information on how to attain these valuable traits. Prospective players who seek to develop these skills gain leverage on the playing field and become the type of player every coach loves to have in the dugout.

Within the pages of *Baseball's Sixth Tool*, you will learn how to become a savvy base runner, smarter pitcher, intuitive hitter, and an offensive defensive player. These tips focus on baseball intelligence inside the game that often separates one player from the next. That separation may be the difference in playing at the high school, college, or professional level.

Baseball is a great game in action and thought. What author Mark Gola enables the reader to experience is not only what players do but what they think, where they look, and how anticipation gives them an advantage over their opponents.

Best of luck in becoming a complete player.

MIKE HAZEN
DIRECTOR OF PLAYER DEVELOPMENT
BOSTON RED SOX

Preface

We are in an age of mechanical genius in baseball. Players articulate and execute the fundamentals of the swing, pitching delivery, and defensive technique with expertise. They learn it all at a very young age from professional instructors at baseball academies and by attending specialized camps. Ask a 10-year-old about the difference between rotational hitting and weight shift hitting, and you may be shocked at the depth of knowledge.

But as strong as these players are at learning and performing proper technique, they are equally deficient in understanding how to play the game. Imagination, daring, creativity, insights—traits that were once described as "baseball instinct"—are all too rare in our modern game of baseball. At times it seems as if baseball *instinct* is nearly *extinct*.

Can baseball instinct be taught and learned? Yes! This new book, *Baseball's Sixth Tool*, was written to help accomplish this task. Whether you're a coach, player, or parent, *Baseball's Sixth Tool* will help you learn to complement the burgeoning physical skills with the instinct to put them to the best use. The book offers 105 tips to assist players who lack instinct, fail to anticipate, and shun risk. Players will become more instinctive by learning where to look, when to look, who to look at, what to listen for, and how to take advantage of this newfound tool.

What is the sixth tool? It's the tool made up of everything except physical ability. Sixth-tool players have exceptional baseball intelligence, a great sense for the game, original thought, and courage. They are constantly using powers of observation to exploit their opponents. The sixth tool makes a player a better base runner without becoming faster, a better pitcher without throwing harder, a better hitter without increasing bat speed, and a better fielder without improving quickness or arm strength. The predecessor to this book, *The Five-Tool Player*, addressed the development of the five essential physical tools in baseball: hitting, hitting for power, arm strength, speed, and defense. Five-tool players are rare, indeed. But sixth-tool players are even scarcer. *Baseball's Sixth Tool* will help you become the complete player, one that every coach is looking for.

Baseball's Sixth Tool is divided into five chapters; the first, "Character," covers personality, or makeup, and how certain character traits are necessary to fully develop the sixth tool. It is one thing, for example, to notice that conditions are right for a delayed steal. It's another thing to do it. The character traits integral to the sixth-tool player are outlined in this chapter.

The chapters that follow discuss specific situations and the innumerable opportunities for the sixth-tool player. Base runners will learn how to advance bases, read pitchers, and capitalize on defensive positioning. Defensive players will understand the importance of being offensive in the field, sense the right time for a pickoff play, and search for "out" opportunities. Pitchers will be taught how to escape jams without throwing a pitch, recognize hitter weaknesses, and improve their bullpen sessions. Hitters will learn to recognize pitch patterns, take advantage of a struggling pitcher, and combat a pitcher who is dominant. All of these tips make the player better without getting bigger, faster, or stronger.

Why Do Today's Players Lack Instinct?

Why is this generation short on playability? Because today's playing environment doesn't include the freedom for young kids to use their minds and develop their intuitive skills. All games are adult supervised and controlled by coaches. Players are told where to stand, when to swing, which pitch to throw, and how big of a lead to take. The same coaches who bemoan a lack of instinct stifle its growth by directing and controlling the players every step of the way throughout a game. Players are trained throughout their careers to listen for an instructive voice and then react. (If Joe Torre is a manager, then many youth coaches are micromanagers.) They aren't afforded the opportunity to listen to the most important voice—the one inside their head that tells them what it sees and feels.

Those who have watched the *Bad News Bears* movies may remember a scene from the second film, *Breaking Training*. The Bears are playing their exhibition game at the Houston Astrodome when their allotted time expires and the game is ended prematurely. The coach of the Bears (Coach Leak) gets out of the dugout and starts a chant that is eventually joined by the entire crowd. He chants, "Let them play! Let them play! Let them play!" Let *them* play. We should all heed those words. It's their game to play.

Players have to be taught at an early age and need direction, but there has to be a happy medium. Adults have to let kids go during the game and *allow them to make mistakes*! Failure is one of the best teaching tools on the baseball field, and kids have to play in an atmosphere in which *it's OK to fail*. That is the only way they'll be able to test their instinct, take risk, and fully realize the power of observation. Playing the game should be challenging and fun! Being told what to do every step of the way strips players of their originality and the game of its creative offerings.

This book helps even out the playing field for those who lack instinctive skills. It concentrates on elements of the game that are rarely explored. Players who read this book will find a lot of the information new and exciting. Hopefully, they have the energy, smarts, and guts to put it to use.

Best of luck in discovering new ways to enjoy playing the game.

Acknowledgments

There are many people who made personal contributions to this publication. For all those who helped me, I'd like to say, "Thanks."

Ron Martirano, editor at McGraw-Hill, for supporting the idea for this book, which is unique in substance and presentation. Thanks for believing in this concept.

Randy Voorhees, developmental editor, for his ideas, guidance, and baseball expertise. This is a book that Randy could have easily written himself, but instead of taking the role of an author, he shared his intelligence and assumed the role of a friend helping a friend.

Michael Plunkett, photographer and friend, for his talents behind the camera and creative input.

Craig Bolt, project editor at McGraw-Hill, for supervising the book's production, bringing drab copy and photos to life.

Mike Hazen, Boston Red Sox director of player development and former Princeton University and minor league baseball player, for writing the Foreword.

Sonny Pittaro, for sitting down for an interview at Fred and Pete's. You're still a great coach, and I'm proud to call you my friend.

Dave Gallagher, for his wealth of baseball knowledge. You need a lot of kid in you to utilize the sixth tool, and Dave will never be accused of being short on juvenile behavior.

Dave Searles, for giving me important feedback during the early stages of the manuscript.

David Reichmann, Erik Mate, and Paul Searles, the three ballplayers who served as models for this book. You were chosen for your blend of baseball ability and character.

My buddies who attended our annual Arizona golf trip—Ed Gola, Bill Hutnik, Britt Calkin, Dave Norris, Jeff Fennelli, and Mark Szalczyk—for teaching me that when faced with a tight deadline, the combination of golf, beers, and writing simply doesn't mix.

Bud Focht, sports information director at Rider University, for supplying me with rosters of the Rider baseball teams from 1991 to 1994.

Koy, for all the little things you did to help me with this book, including the tuna fish sandwich and chips on deadline day. And to Suzanne, for being a great wife to my brother.

My parents, Edward and Paulette Gola, for their support and providing a great life for our family.

1

Character

Why is character a chapter in a book titled *Baseball's Sixth Tool*? Because the sixth tool is entirely about character. It is about being competitive, energetic, aggressive, fearless, observant, and imaginative. These character traits (and many others) embody a player who possesses not only baseball intelligence but also the psychological makeup to put that knowledge to use.

Knowledge is power, and if you know what to look for, the baseball field provides loads of information you can use to your advantage. Once you get that information, what you do with it defines who you are—your character. As an example, let's say you're on second base and your team is rallying.

The pitcher is dealing with assorted emotions and becomes distracted. An individual who plays with only physical tools simply hopes the hitter at bat will drive him in with a base hit. If you're using your sixth tool, you notice that the pitcher isn't changing his looks to second base. He has fallen into a pattern. You capitalize and get a great jump that allows you to steal third base. That stolen base requires intuition, observation, and the courage to act on it. It makes you a special player.

Using your sixth tool means you must play with will. And playing with will includes a willingness to fail, a willingness to be wrong, a willingness to encounter humility, and a willingness to accept responsibility when a bold attempt ends poorly. You are willing to take educated risks because you sense opportunity to capitalize, to take advantage of a situation or player that leads to success. You cannot sit on the sidelines and talk about what you observe and how it might be used to your advantage. You need to get out there and do it.

College Hall of Fame coach Sonny Pittaro had a saying that hung on the wall of his baseball office. It read, "Courage to risk failure is what leads to success." Many players struggle to act on sixth-tool opportunities because their personality doesn't match that type of player. Most sixth-tool players are aggressive, physical, upbeat, risky, competitive, and quick-witted. If these adjectives don't describe you, then you need to undertake an alternate personality on the baseball field. Search and explore that small flame that burns inside you and use the baseball field as your outlet to cut loose. Conservative minds are not intriguing in sports nor do they cause worry. Step outside yourself and play the game for the sake of playing. Do that and the results will begin to fall into place.

This chapter sets the tone for the book. In it, we address ideas and fundamental traits essential to constructing the type of character you will need to execute the tips that fill the following chapters. These traits come more easily to some than to others. You will read about terms such as *resolve*, *awareness*, *imagination*, *body language*, and *gamesmanship* and learn how they are put to use. The tips that are presented in this chapter are not specific to game situations. Several are in the form of a question that will force you to examine yourself and your character.

What Kind of Player Do You Want to Be?

Take out a piece of paper and a pen and write down how you would characterize yourself as a player. This is not an assignment to describe your baseball skills. It is about describing the type of person you are as a baseball player, both good and bad. Are you timid or aggressive? Do you show negative emotion on the field or are you seamless in your composure? Start to formulate a list of words that encapsulate you. Next, write down the type of player you would like to be. You may already possess some of these traits and on some you may fall short.

The point of this exercise is for you to be aware that *there are a lot of things about you as a baseball player that you control, probably more than you think*. You control whether you hustle out onto the field. You control what you're watching and thinking between pitches. You control your work ethic or how much you communicate with teammates. In short, you control *how* you play. By addressing some shortcomings that are within your control, you've outlined a plan to become a better player.

So what kind of player do you want to be? What would you like people to say about you when discussing your character? Think about what an onlooker might say, both positive and negative. If you're a base runner who avoids taking risks, look for opportunities to take extra bases. If you have trouble dealing with failure, make efforts to control your emotions and rebound after an error in the field. If you're trying to develop a changeup but are afraid of how batters will treat it, throw your changeup in the game. Physical tools cannot make you throw that changeup, play with poise, or run the bases with courage. It is the decision to step outside yourself and do it!

Six Character Traits of the Sixth-Tool Player

Players vary in personality just as they differ in their batting stances and pitching deliveries. Some character traits, however, are staples in a sixth-tool player. Six traits in particular spearhead the list of qualities that set a foundation. Sixth-tool players are *competitive, energetic, aggressive, fearless, imaginative,* and *observant.* Each trait is essential but can't stand alone. Each is dependent on the other five. You can't be aggressive without also being observant. Your play will be reckless. An imaginative player needs to be fearless to put that creativity to use. Following are the six significant traits along with a brief description.

Competitive
Inclined, desiring, or suited to compete; to strive consciously or unconsciously for an objective (as position, profit, or a prize)

A competitive player wants to succeed. He will search for a way to conquer through his ability, intellect, and experience, and/or by exploiting weakness. Each small personal gain brings his team closer to triumph. Competitive fire is what drives the bus.

A competitive player takes pride in every at-bat regardless of score, inning, or how he has performed that day. He views each plate appearance as a personal battle between himself and the pitcher. A player who is not competitive gives way if the chips are down or if he has already registered a successful day.

There is nothing wrong with wanting to win. Absolutely nothing. It's symbolic of pride, belief, and a desire to achieve. The primary reason you play sports, hopefully, is because you enjoy it. And there is joy in winning. It would be difficult to find anyone in any facet of life who wouldn't choose winning over losing. In baseball, it's a bonus prize awarded for practice, execution, attentiveness, and effort. Football coaching legend Vince Lombardi has been credited by many for saying, "Winning isn't everything. It's the only thing." Whether Lombardi actually said as much and, if he did, what he meant by it, is the subject of much debate, but one thing we can take from the quote is that there is nothing that replaces the satisfaction of a group of individuals accomplishing a common goal.

Energetic
Operating with marked vigor or effect

Playing baseball with energy is visible proof that the individual is passionate about the game. Those who truly enjoy the game can't hide it, and it's obvious there is nowhere else they would rather be than the baseball field.

An energetic player runs out to his position. A player who lacks energy has to be told to run out to his position.

Hustle and constant activity are telltale signs, but the clearest indication of a player with energy is the look in his eyes. His eyes dance, observe, absorb, and enjoy. Much the way manager Leo Durocher described his legendary player Willie Mays, "He could do the five things you have to do to be a superstar: hit, hit for power, run, throw, and field. And he had that other magic ingredient that runs a superstar into a super, superstar. He lit up the room when he came in. He was a joy to be around."

Ballplayers have two choices. They can play the game in first gear, or they can put it in overdrive. Play the game with mental and physical energy. It will pay dividends, and you'll have fun while you're at it.

Aggressive

Making attacks or encroachments; marked by combative readiness; marked by driving forceful energy or initiative: enterprising

The word *enterprising* is a great word in that definition. It taps into another sixth-tool trait—imagination—but a player who is enterprising is one who is restless in his intent to succeed.

An aggressive player looks for opportunities to slide or dive for a ball. A player who lacks aggression slides or dives only when absolutely necessary.

It's almost without fail that the more aggressive party wins. It's rare that a participant who is passive, lethargic, or apathetic defeats the aggressor. The aggressor knows what he wants and will seek all measures to attain it.

You hear it all the time in baseball. Good hitters "attack the ball." Successful pitchers "go at the hitter." Great base runners are opportunists. Coaches are often heard calling out to fielders, "Come to the ball. Don't let the ball play you." An aggressive baseball player takes the action to the ball, to the pitcher, to the base paths, to the opponent. He does not allow the contending party to take the action to him.

There is a simple quote by Henry David Thoreau, "Kill or be killed." It doesn't get more black and white than that. Do you want to be the one on the offensive, or would you rather sit back and defend or survive? Some show it more than others, but the best players on the diamond are on the hunt.

Fearless

Free from fear; brave

Everyone harbors fears, but sixth-tool players do not allow fear to enter into their minds during competition. It's not something that requires effort; rather, their thoughts are so consumed by images of what can go right that there is no time to consider what might go wrong. At-bats, pitching appearances, ground balls, or attempted steals are chances to do something positive. They are opportunities to help the team or make a memory. Nothing else.

A player who guesses breaking ball on a 2-1 count and rips the pitch in the gap is fearless. The player who senses breaking ball but is concerned about getting jammed on a fastball is succumbing to fearful thoughts of being wrong.

And let's keep something important in mind. Let's say your worst fear imaginable comes true in a game. Is it really that bad? No, it isn't, and do you know why? Because baseball is a game. . . . It's a game! Void of injury, nothing should make you scared. As the late, great boxing mentor Cus D'Amato once said, "The fear of something is usually worse than the reality."

Imaginative

Given to imagining; having a lively imagination; creative ability; showing a command of imagery

If good players are known to anticipate, then creativity would be a means of countering. Part of competing is being unpredictable, and to do that takes imagination. Doing what is expected of you entails experience and training. Doing what is unexpected entails experience and imagination.

An imaginative runner on first base with below-average speed recognizes the game situation and how important it is for him to get into scoring position. He executes a delayed steal and reaches second safely. The runner who lacks imagination remains at first base (understanding his slow foot speed) and hopes the batters knock him around the bases.

Pitchers have patterns, hitters have tendencies, and defenders make decisions based on the situation. An active mind can prey on those certainties when defending and provide an advantage by doing something other than the ordinary on offense.

Imagination enables you to do things that are unusual. It can make you extraordinary. Don't be predictable. Think on your feet while the opponent executes or expects you to execute "by the book."

Observant
Paying strict attention; watchful; keen, perceptive

Former major league player and manager Wes Westrum once said, "Baseball is like church. Many attend, but few understand." People often describe baseball as a boring sport. The knock on it is that there is not enough action and too much time between pitches. But down time is when the chess players get to work. An abundance of information is available to the player. He just has to care to look.

An observant base runner checks the outfield defense and easily goes from first to third when the batter hits a flare to right field. A base runner who does not observe the depth of the outfield must turn to watch the ball, see it drop, and then run. He probably doesn't make it to third base.

In the dugout, out on the field, along the base paths, or on deck, your eyes have to be looking somewhere. You may as well look around to see what you can pick up. Perhaps a pitcher is tipping pitches, or maybe the first baseman is playing deep behind the runner. An opposing base runner might look runnerish and a pitchout is in order. There is an abundance of data available that can be used to your advantage. Learn where to look and when to look for it.

Build Character

The following series of tips address character. They set the table for the qualities needed to execute specific tips in the areas of baserunning, hitting, pitching, and defense. Read and reflect on the commentary and use it to build your sixth-tool foundation.

1. Take advantage of the opponent's human nature.
Baseball is a game of repetition. It is also a humbling game that will test a player's confidence. Because of these factors, players often commit predictable acts based on human nature. Whether it be an act of nonchalant behavior, single-mindedness, or timidity, predict-

able habits that stem from human emotion offer opportunities for a mindful player. Here are a few examples that occur during a baseball game.

- In the example that led off this chapter, a pitcher is having a tough inning. He's getting knocked around and having trouble with the strike zone. You just doubled in a run and are on second base with one out. Whether the pitcher is angry, upset, or nervous, he is distracted. He is much more likely to fall into a pattern of inattentively checking you at second base. This is a time for you to steal third base. Look for the pitcher to look back at you (once or twice) but doing it with a blank stare as if he's going through the motions. Keep a walking lead and take off once his head turns back toward the catcher. This is not as risky as it sounds. It's the safest way to steal third base; it just entails more than your legs.

With a runner on third base and nobody out, keep the ball down in the strike zone. Low strikes generally produce ground balls, and if the batter practices discipline in taking the pitch, it puts you ahead in the count.

- You're the catcher and it's first and second with one out. The runners take off on the pitch for a double steal. If the runner at second appears to have gotten a good jump, throw the ball directly to second base. The tendency for the trail runner is to relax, thinking the play will be at third. He first has to make sure the lead runner breaks, so his jump will be later and less explosive. In addition, he may not run at top speed because he assumes the throw is going to third base. The easy out in this case is at second base. (This is always a good play if the trail runner is slower than the lead runner.)

- You're the pitcher and there's a runner on third with one out in a tie game. The batter is in position to drive in the run and give his team the lead. Often, he'll be anxious to get the barrel out and may lose a degree of discipline at the plate. Pitches just outside of the strike zone and off-speed pitches may lure the hitter into getting himself out. Why give him a pitch and a location he wants when you may be able to exploit his eagerness?

Players get apprehensive, overly aggressive, and inattentive throughout a game. Try to recognize those instances and use the human nature of your opponent to your advantage. Don't spend your time cheering yourself or heckling the opponent. Keep your mind sharply focused on your prey. Human nature is a predictable and exploitable trait.

2. Play the way you would like to be remembered.

Joe DiMaggio was never big on words, but there is one quote that embodies his approach to playing baseball. DiMaggio once said, "There is always some kid who may be seeing me for the first or last time. I owe him my best." DiMaggio was the consummate professional, and that is the way he played each day on every play. He played as if he were making his first and last impression on those watching and his legacy as a player would be determined by the play at hand. Joe DiMaggio played the way he wanted to be remembered.

Very few experience the opportunity of playing before a packed house at Yankee Stadium, but that should not dissuade you from performing your best every time you take the field. Often players are consumed with their own thoughts of how good they are, but when taking the field, consider the thoughts and words others may use when describing your makeup. Do you want to be remembered as a player who hustled on every play or one who couldn't be counted on to hustle all the time? A player who was observant or one who always had to be told? A player who seized the moment in the clutch or buckled under pressure? A player who bounced back from failure or unraveled following a mistake?

The answers to those questions are simple, but players often lose sight of how they play the game and how they are perceived. A great example is a player who goes into a base standing up on a close play rather than sliding. It's inexplicable, but it happens. There is something more to a player who slides into a base hard, even when the play doesn't necessarily require a slide. His actions make a statement about the type of player he is, and the slide places an exclamation point on a positive play.

Derek Jeter and Manny Ramirez are exceptional major league players. Both are blessed with extraordinary talent and have won world championships. When people talk about and remember Jeter, they will describe his physical talents but will quickly supplement those qualities with words like *hustle*, *resolve*, *leadership*, and *winner*. Ramirez will be revered as an phenomenal hitter; *however, . . .* Which player do you want to model yourself after?

Every opportunity you have, play the way you would like to be remembered. You will flourish in the present, help your future, and postmark your memories.

3. Enjoy playing the game.

Do you really like to play baseball? Do you really enjoy the game? If the answer is yes, that's great. Don't be afraid to show it in your play out on the field.

Some players who suit up in a baseball uniform every day don't like playing baseball. They may not admit it or even realize it yet, but it's not an activity they truly enjoy. Whether they're playing because they used to like it when they were much younger, they're simply good at it, or they are out there because Mom or Dad wants them out there, these players are easily identified. And if you are a player who does not like baseball, guess what? It's OK. It doesn't make you a bad person. You should spend your time doing something that you enjoy rather than playing baseball.

For players who do enjoy the game, it's the only way to play. Isn't that why we have games in the first place—to relax and enjoy, to have fun? Play happy. Play excited. Play to win. It's hard to be tense when you're smiling.

"You can tell by watching a player for a few innings whether or not he truly has passion for playing baseball. His body language, his facial expressions, the way he takes the field, or where his attention is between pitches on defense. A player can have all the physical ability in the world, but if he doesn't enjoy playing the game, he's not someone that is attractive to a coach. He's not going to do the little things in a game. He'll dislike practice and probably won't be interested in getting much better. Coaches want players who have passion because you're more likely to have a positive impact on their experience."

—Sonny Pittaro, former college coach and member of the
American Baseball Coaches Association Hall of Fame

Players perform their best when they relax and enjoy themselves. Remember, baseball is a game.

Baseball is a game. Players (and coaches) often need to be reminded of that simple idea. Those who treat it like a game are much more likely to enjoy themselves and excel. Those who approach each game, at-bat, or mound performance as if it will be a life-altering experience will become consumed by frustration because it's a sport of many failures. Remember, the umpire says, "Play ball!"

There is a difference between liking to hit or pitch and enjoying the game. If you really like baseball, you'll find an abundance of opportunities throughout the game where you can be a factor: taking an extra base, preventing a runner from scoring, advancing a runner, or picking a runner off to quell a rally. As baseball author and former college coach Randy Voorhees explains, "When you're enjoying yourself, your mind is clear and you're wide-awake."

Everyone wants to win, and it inspires participants to put forth their very best. But when victory is not the result, it does not diminish the experience of playing, and furthermore, losses often provide greater opportunities to learn and improve. As strange as this sounds, it is sometimes more exhilarating to lose a game 5–4 in extra innings than to win a game 10–0. So many small battles were won and lost within that extra-inning game that it was brimming with excitement. A win or loss is simply an end result to the game. The enjoyable part lies within the time spent out on the field.

People like to be around other people who are happy with what they're doing. It's human nature, and happiness can become contagious. There is an intangible value in a smile. Have fun when you're playing. It will work to your and everyone else's benefit.

4. Be a risk taker.

With the score tied and two outs in the last inning, the batter strokes a line drive over the shortstop's head toward the gap in left center field. The left fielder cuts it off, but the batter knows he has a weak throwing arm. He never stops and attempts to stretch it into a double. Ultimately, the outfielder makes a prefect throw, and he's out at second base.

Was this a costly error in judgment? Absolutely not. The player rolled the dice and this time around, he crapped out.

In this particular situation, the player took an educated risk. And it was the right decision. If he slides in safely, he's in scoring position and needs only a single to score. If he stops at first, it will take two hits (or possibly an extra-base hit) to plate the winning run.

The key element here is that the player was aware that the left fielder had a weak throwing arm and attempted to put that knowledge to use. That is someone who is risk-tolerant. Many players possess the same knowledge but are afraid to apply it. They are risk-averse. They would rather play it safe than take the chance of making what may be *perceived* as a mistake.

In a lot of ways, baseball is a game of playing the odds. There are gambles in how you position yourself in the field, what pitch to look for in a count, what pitch to throw to a batter, and when to try to steal a base. If you trust your baseball intelligence (and your sixth tool), you will be right much more often than wrong. Trust what your gut is telling you and act on it. Remember, without taking some risk, there will never be a major reward.

Being risk-averse does not make you a bad player, but it makes you ordinary. You want to be a player who does things that are unusual on the baseball field. Make plays that force onlookers to stop and say, "Wow, did you see what he did on that play?"

Too often in baseball, risk is frowned upon. It's often an impulse decision by the player that goes against the grain of conventional thinking. That means it lies outside of the control of the coach. Never forget, the game is not played by the coaches. It's played by the players. Taking that calculated risk is what can make you exceptional. Don't allow coaches to strip you of tenacious play.

There is an element of fear in risk. That's what makes it fun. That fear makes you run a little faster or equips you with more strength, quickness, or fight. It should not stop you from making a play. That makes you ordinary.

5. Play with fire.

Because baseball is a game of high-level skill, technique is very important. No coach would shun a player who is blessed with physical tools. But it takes more than ability. As the great hitting instructor Charlie Lau once explained, "Nothing is more common than unsuccessful men with talent." Playing the game with enthusiasm, excitement, and energy brings out the best in a player.

Have you ever seen Vladimir Guerrero run the bases? He looks like an uncaged lion that has just been released from captivity. His body language is one of sheer determination, and his facial expressions are not those of someone who plans to be denied. That hustle and physical presence are the results of a player who has made a mental and emotional commitment to playing the game with tenacity. When you play this way, you are free of worry and full of pride. Try to somehow involve yourself in every play on the field. View pressure situations as opportunities.

Playing with fire is a decision. It is something you control. Every light switch is turned on from head to toe and available to illuminate a path that leads you toward defeating an opponent. Philadelphia Phillies second baseman Chase Utley is a perfect example of someone who plays with fire. He's a five-tool player, but what makes him a superstar is his passionate approach to playing.

It's important to understand that playing with fire does not mean going crazy. If you think about Utley, he dives for balls, runs hard, slides aggressively, but at the plate, he's very calm. His thoughts and concentration are intense, but his body is relaxed. This is essential

An aggressive slide is symbolic of who you are and how you play.

in being able to slow the game down and think while your body acts explosively.

When you play with fire, you're easy to pick out on a baseball field and you'll make a lasting impression on those watching. It will be impossible not to notice your enthusiasm. So charge out onto the field when taking your position. Talk to your teammates. Slide hard into a base even when a slide may not be necessary. Make every part of your game noticeable and keep your mind working, imagining, anticipating what is next. Playing with fire is controlled 100 percent by the person in the mirror. Be on the plus side of this trait, not the downside.

6. Play to make plays rather than playing to not make mistakes.

While this tip may not sound eloquent, it speaks volumes about the personality of a player and his ability to perform. With regard to this subject, the game has two divisions of players: those who play to excel and those who spend nine innings trying to avoid mistakes. The first set presents a challenge to the opposition. The second set is primed for exploitation. As Hall of Famer Lou Brock once said, "Show me a guy who's afraid to look bad, and I'll show you a guy you can beat every time."

Always take the field in search of opportunities to do something special. Look to charge a slow roller and throw off the wrong foot, lace a first-pitch fastball in the gap, or stretch a single into a double. These plays require courage, desire, and imagination. They make people take notice. You do not want to catch yourself thinking, for example, "If I swing at a first-pitch fastball and make an out, I'll be questioned by myself and several others." That thought of failure cannot enter into the equation. The better train of thought is, "This guy has been throwing a fastball for strike one all game. If I get a good fastball, I'm going to punish the pitch."

Fearing mistakes will not only bring on those miscues more frequently, but also you'll never make those special plays that require a relaxed and open mind. As the cliché goes, "Nothing ventured, nothing gained." Delayed steals, pickoff plays, and bunt base hits are momentum-shifting plays that positive-minded players enjoy. Using the sixth tool enables you to sit on a breaking pitch, to throw

The best defensive players want the ball hit to them. They're cocksure the result will be an out.

a changeup in a fastball count, and to throw behind the runner after receiving the cutoff. Although you might get fooled and freeze on a fastball, your changeup may miss the strike zone, and your throw could get away from a teammate who's not expecting the throw, you must be able to accept those temporary failures in order to experience the heights of risk-reward play.

7. Practice as you play.

Baseball is a game of repetition, and to build confidence and polish your skills, practice is a necessity. But how do you practice? Do you coast through at 75 percent to get your work in, or do you train at game speed? Any coach will tell you that a 60-minute practice that is mentally and physically challenging has greater value than a 120-minute practice that goes through the motions.

Taking ground balls in the infield is a good example. Anyone can field ground ball after ground ball hit to him. Change the pace or direction of the hit and add a base runner and now you've simulated game conditions. Baseball is not a light-switch game. Don't expect to speed things up and execute with consistency if you haven't been practicing it at an accelerated rate. In this game the body and mind need to perform relaxed so they can react efficiently. If you train at game speed during practice, you'll be less likely to tense up in a game. You relax when you're familiar with the conditions.

A great way to sustain quality practice is to create mini contests or competitions among teammates. Place a winner at the end of each exercise and the intensity and focus will take care of itself. You'll not only practice at game speed, but you'll actually have fun doing it as well.

8. Act as if you've been there.

Baseball can provide some exciting moments. Extra-base hits, diving plays in the field, and striking a hitter out are just a few examples. When these positive plays happen, act like you've been there before. Carry yourself like a winner. Composure is a valuable trait in the light of success, not just in dire situations.

After a home run, double play, or team victory, don't carry on excessively. Enjoy the moment, embrace the satisfaction, and then move forward. Great players and teams never get too high and never get too low.

9. Always respect the umpire. Make him a fan, not a foe.

By observing the actions of many coaches and parents (adults), players develop a senseless and illogical distaste for umpires. It is a part of amateur baseball that is shameful and continues to worsen. Respect the umpires because it's the right thing to do, but also because it's a sixth-tool trait that can benefit your game.

There are several good reasons to respect the umpire and his role in the game. First, without a game official, there is no game. Period. It's a fact that many forget once the game starts. Leagues scramble to schedule umpires, and coaches and parents are anxious for the umpire to arrive at the game site so they know the contest will be played. Once the game starts, however, that valued figure is often villainized. It's a common occurrence that is simply baffling.

From a sixth-tool standpoint, you want the umpire on your side. When your team witnesses the opponent complaining to or berating the ump, recognize it as an advantage to your team. Umpires are human beings and, by nature, the actions of the participants can influence their judgment on a call that could go either way. Whether it's a borderline strike or a bang-bang play at first base, an umpire is more likely to make a favorable call to a respectful player than to one who mouths off in protest when a call doesn't go his way.

You will always think you're right when judging balls and strikes. Everyone does. Understand that your interpretation of the strike zone must take a backseat to the umpire's version of the strike zone. He is the authority figure for that day. View the umpire's strike zone as a component to the game, rather than fighting him on what he thinks is a ball or strike. When a pitcher is warming up, hitters look to "see what he has." Look at the umpire the same way. What is his strike zone? Is it high or low? Does he squeeze the pitcher? Once you accept the fact that it's his strike zone, you can channel all of your mental energy into the game and opponent instead of being distracted by disagreeing with the game official. Let the other team do that.

Again, showing respect can be rewarded if you don't react negatively to the call being made. A pitcher may get a call in a future count or the hitter may receive a break during an at-bat later in the game. Cutting comments, bad body language, or combative glares will likely get the strike zone to shrink or expand, whichever works against the argumentative player.

10. Communicate with your teammates to make them better.

If you have knowledge, share it with your teammates. It can make a positive difference in that game, a future game, and the personality of your team.

The power of observation can provide you with additional ammunition during competition. Knowing the tendencies of an opposing hitter, getting a good jump on the pitcher, or picking up signs is great information that must be passed along to teammates. Spread that wealth of information because it increases your team's chances of success.

An opposing pitcher, for example, may be tipping his pitches. If you pick up on it (and make absolutely sure you're correct), tell your teammates. Wouldn't you want to know if a breaking ball is coming? It can mean the difference between a win and a loss.

The cool thing that can happen with a team is that everyone starts looking for small advantages to pick up on every game. It becomes part of the team's identity. Not everyone takes pride in being smart in the classroom, but all players like the feeling of being known as a savvy baseball player.

11. "Thou shalt steal."

Stealing signs can be a controversial topic in baseball. The real question is, why? If a team can pick up predictable signs that the opponent fails to adequately disguise, so be it. It's gamesmanship. A player or team that has signals stolen should spend their energy coming up with a better system, rather than griping about their opponents. If you can steal signs, steal them. Just don't get caught. (With all due respect to Bill Belichick and the New England Patriots, videotaping opponents is taking things a little too far.)

When college coach Randy Voorhees played for Mercer County Community College in the Junior College World Series, his team stole signs the entire game. The theft was fairly simple, and the communication of those signs was a team effort. It went like this: The opposing catcher gave the sign to his pitcher. The second baseman reached behind his back and relayed what pitch was coming to the outfielders. Behind the outfielders, however, were the Mercer pitchers seated in the bullpen. They took the sign from the opposing second baseman and signaled the on-deck hitter of the next pitch. The on-deck hitter then gave a verbal sign to the hitter to let him know what pitch was coming.

As with any theft, it is important not to get caught with your hand in the cookie jar. The consequences can be painful. If opponents catch on to you stealing signs, they may cross you up. They'll call for something soft away to get you leaning out over the plate, and guess what's coming? A fastball tight or at you. Whether they target the hip, the back, or the chin depends on who you're dealing with and the game situation.

Stealing signs isn't just about learning the signals from the third-base coach or the individual in the dugout calling pitches. You can sense that a play is coming based on the body language of the player, coach, or players in the dugout. Coaches will have a certain rhythm or intensity going through a set of signs when a play is being called. The facial expressions of the players involved may get more attentive, intense, or show disappointment (such as when given a sacrifice

If an opposing coach has predictable sign sequences, that lies on him. Use it to your team's advantage.

bunt sign). Players in the dugout may whisper to each other when they see a sign given for an upcoming play.

One play for which you may observe several giveaways is the suicide squeeze. When it's late in the game, the score is tied or within a run, and a weaker hitter is at the plate, look for one or more of the following tip-offs that indicate a squeeze might be on.

- Third-base coach whispers to the runner on third at any point during the at-bat.
- Third-base coach makes sure he has the attention of both the hitter and the base runner before starting his signs.
- Third-base coach is very deliberate running through his sequence of signs.
- Batter gives an acknowledgment signal to verify he has received the sign. This could be sliding his hands up the bat, tapping his cleats with the bat, fastening his helmet, and so on.

- Batter displays body language that he is nervous or disappointed.
- Batter moves up in the box and closer to home plate (as he is taught to do in this situation).
- Batter's routine or stance isn't the same. It's stiff or somehow doesn't appear as if he's preparing to hit.
- Players in the dugout are whispering to each other.
- Entire dugout gets quiet.
- Runner on third base has a bigger lead or looks runnerish.

12. Resolve produces results.

Part of what makes baseball a great sport is its degree of difficulty. It's a tremendous challenge, which is why many develop such passion for the game. Failure should never be accepted or enjoyed, but the high rate of failure forces competitors to retool and seek retribution—that is, if they have resolve.

Resolve is a must in this sport. The game will test your fortitude, and without it, you'll succumb to its ruthless nature and fail to experience consistent success. At younger levels, physical talent can stand up to the rigors of baseball. The longer the game is played, however, the better the players are and the more the game speeds up. Your emotional and psychological strength become increasingly significant.

Resolve is called on when you're on the mound and can't find the strike zone; when you're 0-for-3 and have two strikes in the count in your fourth at-bat; when you get the steal sign and were thrown out in your previous attempt. You depend on your resolve when the chips are down and the odds are stacked against you. When you're searching for that strike zone, you need to self-correct and find it or figure out some other way to get an out and survive the inning (a pickoff play, for example). If the resolve well is dry, it won't be long before the manager is on his way out to the mound to take the ball.

Great players go to another place when things aren't going their way. They push aside the peripheral elements and focus on what they need to be successful. A strong resolve allows a player to forget what has happened and fight for what needs to get done.

13. Be a player who has to win.

Winning isn't everything, but there is nothing wrong with wanting to win. There is great satisfaction to competing against a valid opponent and emerging victorious. Simply stated, it's more gratifying than losing.

There is a special category of athletes who have to win. Whitey Ford, Bob Gibson, Pedro Martinez, and John Smoltz are examples of pitchers who possess a mean streak when it comes to winning. Tiger Woods and Michael Jordan are examples of must-win athletes in other sports. Certain players (at all levels) seem to want it more than others. Every fiber of their body is about coming out ahead. These players aren't necessarily the most talented, and they likely wouldn't achieve what they do without that passion to succeed. That personality trait can make an ordinary player a special player. As former major league manager Fred Mitchell once said, "The spirit to win is worth 20 points to any batting average and an additional pitcher to any club."

Josh Schwartz was a pitcher at Rowan University from 2002 to 2005. During his career, he won 37 consecutive games. (That's an NCAA record for all divisions of baseball.) Any way you shake it, it's an incredible feat. Coaches who opposed Schwartz agree that he was a quality pitcher, but the lasting impression they had of him was that as soon as you got him in trouble, he would elevate his game to a higher level. Once runners were aboard and the opponent threatened to rally, he became increasingly stubborn and difficult with his pitches. His will to win was as much of a weapon as his sharp, left-handed curveball.

After Schwartz threw a complete-game shutout for his 37th consecutive win against Hampden-Sydney College in the first round of the Division III College World Series, Hampden-Sydney coach Jeff Kinne said, "He had something up his sleeve for everything we tried to do. He just knows how to pitch." His left arm receives the credit, but his heart is an equal factor. It's an intangible that often goes unnoticed and underappreciated.

Wins, just like base hits at times, don't always have to be pretty. Sometimes you have to win ugly, and those types of wins are so important to your overall makeup. There will be certain battles in which you'll triumph purely based on ability. But other times, whether it be that your game is off or the opponent is physically superior, you have to figure out ways to win. That's what separates the good from the great.

14. "It's not how hard you hit, it's how hard you can get hit and keep moving forward."

Apologies to Sylvester Stallone and the Rocky Balboa character for heisting this line, but it's a great thought that is ideal for baseball players. The game throws the book at you in terms of slumps, errors, strikeouts, and costly mistakes. Time after time, baseball will knock you to the canvas. The question is, are you able to pick yourself up and continue to fight?

Professional baseball scouts assess physical strengths and weaknesses in young prospects, but character makeup also plays a large role. If a scout has interest in a player, he would actually like to see him struggle in some aspect of a game to see how he responds. It serves as a window into the future of how a prospect will respond during inevitable tough times. Minnesota Twins scout John Wilson says, "There are three makeup questions that I'll try to answer when scouting a player: (1) How will he handle failure? (2) Does he have the ability to make adjustments? (3) Does he have the makeup to survive the minor leagues? The minor leagues are a tough lifestyle, and it takes mental and emotional strength to make it."

The ability to put mistakes behind you and maintain confidence is extremely important. Throwing helmets, taking your bat with you onto the field (mentally), and arguing with umpires are examples of players responding poorly to failure. Negative thoughts and actions about what *has* happened do not allow the player to think clearly about what he *needs to do next*. A player who lacks emotional stability will have difficulty playing baseball at higher levels.

Most collegiate and professional prospects have experienced an enormous amount of success playing baseball throughout their lives. They were all stars on their Little League teams, in middle school, in high school, and on up the chain. They have encountered limited situations in which they've struggled or looked bad. At some point, the playing field balances out and the pitchers, hitters, and defensive players they're up against get really good. Churning out hits, throwing out base runners, or collecting strikeouts doesn't come quite so easily, and it tests the true character of the player. "A player needs

As a pitcher, there will be games when the hitters knock you around. You can feel sorry for yourself, or look at it as an opportunity to show your mettle.

legitimate confidence and mental toughness to deal with failure," notes Baylor University head coach Steve Smith.

How you act and carry yourself when you succeed is the easy part. It's during the tough times you have to show grit and battle. You will get knocked down in baseball. The question is will you have the pride, poise, and spirit to get up and stand tall.

15. It takes no talent to hustle.

Run to your position. Run off the field. Sprint down the first-base line on pop-ups and fly balls. Slide into the base on close plays. Back up throws in the infield and outfield. Make aggressive turns on the base paths.

These are situations that you control as a player. They are a reflection of your character, personal pride, and passion for the game. We all know how a lack of hustle can make you look bad, so let's talk about a few examples of how good hustling can make you look instead.

- A player who hustles earns the respect of his teammates, coaches, umpires, opponents, and spectators.
- A player who hustles will rub off on a few teammates and have a positive impact on their playing careers.
- Hustle will make a player feel good about himself.
- Hustle can turn a short fly ball into a double.
- A player who hustles to back up a play can bail out a teammate who made a mistake and also make himself look smart.
- A player who hustles on defense can get to a ball thought to be unreachable and get his pitcher out of a jam.
- Hustle can make the difference in winning a baseball game.

There is no better example of hustle and how good it can make you look than what Derek Jeter pulled off in the 2001 divisional playoff series against the Oakland Athletics. The A's held a two games to none lead over the Yankees.

Holding a 1–0 lead in the seventh inning, pitcher Mike Mussina yielded a base hit to Jeremy Giambi. Terrence Long then came to the plate and laced a two-out double down the right-field line. With two outs, Giambi attempted to score from first base.

Yankees right fielder Shane Spencer uncorked a throw that sailed over the head of first-base cutoff Tino Martinez. Giambi never broke stride rounding third, but by seeing the ball thrown out of the reach of Martinez, he may have relaxed and slowed up.

Jeter had no assigned responsibilities for the play, but as Spencer prepared for a long throw, he raced over to first to back up Martinez. He fielded the errant throw on one bounce, then flipped the ball backhand to catcher Jorge Posada in midstride, and Posada tagged Giambi (who failed to slide) out at the plate. The Yankees held on for a 1–0 victory and went on to win the series three games to two.

Jeter looked incredibly smart and passionate on that play. He figured out a way to positively impact the game on a play in which he had virtually no role. He observed, he anticipated, and then he acted. That play embodies a sixth-tool player.

Hustle is a word constantly preached by coaches. But don't do it for them. Do it for yourself. It will make you feel superior and contribute to your team's play.

Running on and off the field demonstrates your respect for the game and, even more important, self-respect.

16. Be confident, not cocky.

Anyone will tell you that confidence is essential to success on the baseball field. Confidence allows players to relax (physically and mentally), to take risks, to take the offensive rather than playing in survival mode. What do they say about players in the field who don't want the ball hit to them? The ball will somehow find them.

While a high level of confidence is a common trait in great athletes, it is best to play with quiet confidence. You have a right to foster brash thoughts, but they should not be outwardly displayed. It can be disrespectful to the opposition, and more often than not, showboating is a sign of personal insecurity, not confidence. Confident players know they're good. They don't need to flaunt it.

Confident players have a presence about them. They carry an aura that emanates self-assurance and certainty. It's the imposing presence a pitcher has on the mound, the way a hitter goes through his prestance routine, or the manner in which a third baseman fields a ground ball. Each is like a mountain lion perched in a tree quietly waiting to pounce on its prey.

You know cocky players when you see them. They perform as if a camera is capturing their every move and the game is all about them. Flamboyance and trash-talking are practiced by those who seek attention, nothing more. In general, no one likes a cocky person. It's a turnoff in any facet of life. Teammates will lose some respect for you and opponents will want to go above and beyond to defeat you.

Remember, it's quiet confidence that you seek. Confidence is a feel, not a show.

17. Do unto others as you would have others do unto you.

You have been there and you will be there again. Remember what a lonely place it can be. You have struck out looking. You have thrown a ball away that allowed runs to score. You have missed the cutoff man. You have missed a sign. You have been picked off. You have had trouble finding the strike zone. You have taken a swing at a high fastball.

When you've committed one of these acts of error, you have felt the emptiness of personal failure. You have also felt that you have hurt or endangered your team's chances of winning. It doesn't help or make you feel any better when a teammate lays into you. You felt bad enough already and now you feel worse.

When one of these common mistakes happens to a teammate, keep the golden rule in mind. Do not yell at him, do not ostracize him, and do not make comments to another teammate about him. It will make that player feel worse and, with that, heighten the chances of him making a follow-up mistake. If anything, make eye contact with him and tell him to forget about it. "Hey, get the next one. Don't worry about it. We need you to get the next one." Make his future play seem valuable. That will give him a sense for a chance at redemption.

A perfect example of this is when a batter swings at a pitch in the dirt for strike three and breaks for first base. The catcher blocks the ball, picks it up, and makes an errant throw to first base, allowing the runner to be safe. As the pitcher, you're disappointed and rightfully so. It does no good, however, to show negative emotion. You *need* that catcher to be at his best to receive pitches, block balls, and throw out runners for the remainder of the game. And remember, whenever you're in trouble, he trots out to the mound to give you support.

Make it a point to calmly tell the catcher to shake it off. Say, "Great block." Don't turn your back on him and avoid eye contact. Be demonstrative in support and go back to work. The catcher will appreciate it and respond with his play.

You have been there and will be there again. Remember what a lonely place it can be.

You can absorb a tremendous amount of information in baseball by simply paying attention in the dugout.

2
Baserunning

Baserunning is the least sexy element of baseball, perhaps because most players don't think of themselves as fast enough to be good base runners. It's a part of the game that is seldom emphasized and one that welcomes uninhibited imagination, bravery, and sophistication. Hitting will get you to the dance floor, but once you're there, you need to observe, create, and go after home plate. As college coach Gordie Gillespie once said, "There are 26 ways to score from third base. Get there!"

A memorable film clip is played every July during the week leading up to the major league All-Star Game. It's footage of Pete Rose in the 1970 summer classic played in Cincinnati. In the bottom of the 12th inning, the score was tied 4–4 with two out and Rose on second base. Jim Hickman singled, and Rose raced around third base determined to score. American League catcher Ray Fosse moved up the line to receive the throw, and Rose lowered his shoulder and pounded Fosse into the turf to jar the ball loose and score the winning run. It was an act of bravery and determination by Rose.

Both Rose and Fosse were injured on the play (Fosse more seriously), and it remains a topic of controversy to this day. Think and say what you want about Rose, but that is how he played. That is how he ran the bases. Rose could not turn the faucet on or off depending on the setting. He ran the bases as if he were being chased and his only hope for survival was to reach home safely. Rose wasn't the fleetest of foot, but he was a terrific base runner. When you think of how you want to run the bases, think of Pete Rose.

How do you become a better base runner without improving foot speed? By utilizing the sixth tool. Using your eyes and embracing a willingness to take risk can catapult you from being a below-average base runner to being an above-average one. By being observant, aggressive, and imaginative, you have endless opportunities to excel. The base paths will become your personal playground.

In reading this chapter, you'll be exposed to information that will improve your baserunning. These tips do not discuss running form, explosive first steps, or sliding techniques. They teach you to understand the game situation from the base paths, read defenses, sense pitch patterns, and anticipate textbook defensive execution or lapses in the defense's concentration. It's how runners get good jumps, take extra bases, and swipe a bag without a throw. This information, however, is not enough. You've got to put it to use.

A sixth-tool base runner has a presence that is felt by the defense. His impact on the field is both direct and indirect. The direct is easy to pick out, but the indirect effect is what often goes unnoticed. Drawing attention from the pitcher, catcher, and infield lessens the focus on the hitter. The catcher is distracted in calling pitches and how he receives them. The infielders will cheat toward bases leaving wider hitting lanes for the batter. And most important, the pitcher is much more vulnerable to making a mistake with his pitch. When a pitcher is rushing his delivery with less focus on locating his pitch or trying to prevent a breaking pitch in the dirt, that works to the advantage of the hitter.

Achieving the Ultimate Goal: Score!

Ask any player this question: "If you get up to the plate and lace a line-drive base hit, are you successful?"

My guess is that 99.9 percent of the players will answer yes. The response is understandable, but it falls short of the larger picture. The better answer is, "I've cleared the first hurdle by getting on base, but I haven't attained success until I've crossed home plate." That is the type of player a team cherishes. That is a player who is willing to employ a sixth tool. The base hit, while gratifying, is important because it positions the player to reach the ultimate goal: scoring a run. Now what does that player need to do to get home?

Players have a tendency to become complacent when they get a hit. That is a primary source of weakness from which base runners suffer. They need to stay hungry and explore every opportunity to advance. A team that undertakes this approach on the base paths will force mistakes and score runs. They will not be so dependent on a series of hits to push them to home plate.

A secondary, yet very influential source of poor baserunning is fear. Players fear getting thrown out stealing, being picked off, or getting cut down attempting to take an extra base. That is no way to run the bases. Good base runners are greedy, and when they stick a base in their back pocket, they immediately seek out the next one.

A conservative approach on the bases, or "playing it safe," can cost a team runs just as easily as an errant throw on defense. The only difference is the conservative baserunning mistake doesn't show up in the box score. A base runner on first with a station-to-station approach who stops at second on a base hit to right field when he could have reached third with one out is guilty of an egregious error. When the next hitter to take the plate flies out to deep center field, that base runner cost his team a run. Again, it simply doesn't show up in the box score.

As the base runner, you are not satisfied until you touch home plate and get a run on the scoreboard.

Playing the Odds: Taking Calculated Risks

Baserunning is an environment for oddsmakers. There are wagers everywhere and courageous players like to roll the dice. That is not to suggest a player is to perform with reckless abandon, but he should test the limits.

Jose Reyes is one of the most dangerous base stealers in the game today. He'll also be near (or at) the top of the list of runners getting picked off. And that doesn't include all the times he nearly gets picked off. It's not a coincidence. Reyes recognizes that without the risk of an aggressive lead, he won't be a legitimate baserunning threat.

In playing the odds on the bases, a player can find more than one way to come out ahead. Think about it. A runner who risks taking an extra base, for example, has three ways he can slide into a base safely. The first is simply that his decision was correct. He came out on the plus side of the risk. The second is that the urgency and excitement of the play forces physical error: an errant throw, poor positioning by the baseman, or any simple failure in execution. The third is the defense is completely caught off guard by the risk and no play is made at all. Defensive players often think the baserunning game through their own conservative minds, and in this case, they fail to anticipate an aggressive baserunning move. Somebody on the field will not be in position to make the play.

Observation before the play occurs minimizes risk. There still may be a degree of risk, but it's an educated risk. A player who goes first to third on a base hit through the first-base hole may have already considered that the right fielder is a right-handed thrower and is shaded toward the right-center-field gap. He will have to run away from his throwing side, which takes the player more time to field the ball and will likely reduce his arm strength and/or accuracy. Going from first to third is now a calculated risk.

Tips for Base Runners

The following tips focus on teaching base runners where, when, and what to look for on the baseball field. There is ample time between pitches, and instinctive base runners use this time to collect as much data as possible. Remember, an aggressive base runner creates offense and finds ways to advance and score. A complacent base runner depends on the offense of others.

1. Use your eyes, not your ears, to run the bases.

A runner is on first base with one out. The batter drives a base hit to left-center field. The base runner rounds second and heads for third, despite the fact that his third-base coach is telling him to hold.

Is the runner wrong? No, he sees the play right in front of him and thinks he can make third base safely.

This generation of youth players has grown up in a baseball society that is micromanaged. Teams are equipped with four to six coaches who are rarely at a loss for words or direction. Most players today learn to run the bases by listening to what they hear as opposed to trusting and reacting to what they see. Good base runners use their base coaches only as a very last resort. Poor base runners are dependent on their base coaches. When a coach has to instruct a runner to go, often it's already too late. As aptly put by former major leaguer Dave Gallagher, "Good base runners only need a coach to stop them. Bad base runners need a coach to make them go."

Playing pickup games is where players of past generations developed their baserunning instincts. There was little or no supervision, so no one was telling them what they could or could not do. This is where players learned what was a mild risk, a risk, or too much of a risk. If they failed and were thrown out, they learned from their mistake. It's much like learning to maximize the length of a lead. You never know how much is too much until you get picked off (or nearly picked off). Failure is often the best way to learn how close to the edge you can get without falling off.

Today, players are conditioned to lead and run at the peril of an adult's voice. "Go," "Hold up," "Back," "Get more," "One step back," "Go to second," "Stay at third." Base runners are nothing but mere puppets in a game controlled by adults. And when coaches witness a lack of instinct or aggressiveness on the base paths, they wonder why.

2. On second base, always know where the shortstop is playing.

A runner takes his secondary lead off second base. The batter rips a line drive directly at the base runner. The runner immediately breaks full speed toward third base and easily scores on the base hit.

How did he know the ball wouldn't be caught? He knew precisely where the shortstop was positioned when the ball was struck.

Former major leaguer Dave Gallagher recalls how he was heralded by his teammates for this type of play several times during his career.

"I can remember the same type of play happening a few times when the hitter got sawed off and hit a soft line drive toward shortstop. I broke immediately and scored, never looking back to see if the ball was caught or not. Guys in the dugout would tell me, 'Man, Gally, that took guts. That's a big risk you took.'

"I thought to myself, 'No, it wasn't. I knew exactly where the shortstop was and knew he had no chance of catching the ball.' You do have to trust yourself on that play, but when you score easily, you look like a very instinctive base runner."

Checking to see where the shortstop is playing helps you recognize when you can advance to third on a ground ball, when the ball will get through so you can bow into your turn toward home, and when to hold. What is important is that you glance back using peripheral vision as you complete your secondary lead. Knowing where the shortstop is before the pitch is not always an indication of where he will be when the ball enters the hitting zone.

On a routine ground ball to shortstop, you're taught by coaches to break for third if the ball is "at you or to your left." That is the rule. However, if you already know the shortstop is shaded up the middle (defending a left-handed pull-hitter for example), then you may even advance to third on a routine ground ball to your right.

Lastly, you give yourself a chance to get back to second base on a line drive directly at the shortstop. If the ball is hit to where the shortstop is positioned, break back to the base as soon as you see the ball's flight.

3. Always check the outfielders' positioning: depth and shading.

A below-average runner stands on first base. The number five hitter gets fisted and drops a short fly ball into right field. Despite having limited running speed, the base runner ends up on third base without drawing a throw.

How did he accomplish this so easily? He wanted to go from first to third on a hit, and he observed conditions that would allow it to happen.

When on first or second base (especially first base), glance back to see where the outfielders are positioned. Take note of how deep they're playing and whether they're playing straight up or shaded toward the gap or line.

DEEP OUTFIELD DEFENSE. An outfielder playing deep makes it easier to eat up two bags on a base hit. There is great value in going first to third on a base hit, so if an outfielder is guarding the deep ball, there should be no hesitation. Approach second base at top speed and continue to the next. You should glance up at the third-base coach if the ball is behind you (right or right-center field), but remember, the base coach is only there to stop you, not to keep you coming.

Balls hit deep to the gap, however, are not automatic. You may have to turn to the outfield to get a sense of whether the outfielder will make the play. Knowing the outfielder's running speed and range before this happens is helpful. When you're on first base, go all the way to second base if the ball is taking the outfielder away from first base. If it takes him toward first base, your distance from first base depends on your running speed and the outfielder's arm strength.

From second base, leave yourself the option to tag up with nobody out. If the ball drops in safely, you'll still be able to score on the play. Your judgment is critical in this situation. If the outfielder appears destined to catch the ball, get back and tag. If not, get close enough to the base to tag, but far enough to score on the hit.

SHALLOW OUTFIELD DEPTH. An outfield that plays shallow makes it difficult for the base runner to advance two bases on a single, but it is not impossible. The location of the hit may force the outfielder to go to his right or left. In this case, knowledge of whether the outfielder is right-handed or left-handed is useful information. On balls hit away from his throwing side (a ball that forces a right-handed thrower to move to his left and vice versa), you may have a good chance of taking two bases. Again, outfielder arm strength and your speed are factors.

If a batter drives a ball for distance, you're off to the races—you think about nothing but scoring. If you're unaware of the outfield depth, you'll be forced to turn to the outfield, look, and see that the ball is going to beat the defensive player. That hesitation may cause you to be held up at third by the coach. He who hesitates is lost.

BASE RUNNER'S CHECKLIST ON OUTFIELDERS
- Outfielder's depth
- Is the outfielder straight away or shaded?
- Right-handed or left-handed thrower
- Playing surface (length of grass, synthetic turf)
- Wind
- All three outfielders' arm strength and mobility/range

A right-handed right fielder takes more time to throw the ball when he makes a catch moving to his left. Take this into consideration as the base runner.

4. In a first-and-third situation, when the runner from first breaks, the runner on third fakes stealing home.

In a first-and-third situation, the runner on first breaks for second. The defense decides to throw the ball through to second base but will cut the ball off if the runner from third breaks. The runner on third does break, but then holds and returns to third. The first-base runner slides into second safely uncontested.

Why did the runner from third break? He anticipated the infield defense on the first-and-third situation.

Here is what you can do on third base to help the runner attempting to steal second in this situation. First, shorten your primary lead off third base on the pitch. When the ball is thrown through to second, break (three or four hard jab steps) toward home. This will force the middle infielder covering to leave the base and cut the ball off. Slam on the brakes and quickly return to third base. The base runner stealing second base will slide in safely uncontested.

This is a little thing; however, it all but guarantees the runner going to second will slide in safely. Now there are two runners in scoring position. It's simply a matter of knowing how the opponent is going to defend the play and then exploiting that plan. It's countering their counter to the first-and-third steal. Because the runner on third is closer to home, he's of greater concern to the middle infielders. Any motion toward home will draw the middle infielder in and off the second-base bag.

In this situation, you're not doing anything on third base, so why not fake a break and help your teammate reach second?

5. Don't freeze on a line drive at third base—get back!

With the bases loaded, the batter drills a line drive that is caught by the shortstop. The shortstop quickly throws to third base for the double play, but the runner gets back safely.

Why didn't the runner at third get doubled off? He didn't freeze on the line drive.

With a runner on third base, the all-too-common words from the third-base coach are, "Fly ball back to the base, make sure the ground ball goes through, and freeze on a line drive."

Why freeze? With an aggressive secondary lead, you're vulnerable to being doubled off, especially if the ball is hit to the left side of the infield. Get back on a line drive. If the ball goes through, you can trot home.

6. The delayed steal is executed with brains, eyes, and guts.

A below-average runner is on first base and takes a conservative lead. The pitch is thrown, and in midflight, the runner breaks for second base. The catcher receives the pitch and the runner ultimately slides into second base without drawing a throw.

How could he steal without a throw from the catcher? He took advantage of a defense asleep at the wheel.

The greatest advantage a slow runner has is that the defense often fails to pay attention to him on the bases. It is only an advantage, however, when the runner demonstrates the courage and gamesmanship to put it to use.

The delayed steal is built for slow-footed base runners. It's a play that requires observation and timing to pull off. In terms of obser-

On a line drive off the bat, get back to the base. If the ball goes through, you'll score easily.

vation, stay attentive to the middle infielders and the catcher. When the second baseman and shortstop are not shaded toward second base and not pinching toward second after the pitch is received, they are vulnerable to a delayed steal. Keep in mind that middle infielders will glance to the runner at first as the pitcher lifts his leg. When they see the runner shuffle into a secondary lead, their attention goes 100 percent to the plate.

With regard to catchers, they typically have their rear end higher in their catcher's stance with a speedy runner on first base. A slow-footed runner enables them to sit lower in their squat and focus on receiving (and framing) pitches. It's very easy to notice when a catcher is too relaxed and susceptible to a delayed steal. Also, when he does not hear the call "Going!" or "Runner!" on the pitch, he'll relax even further and focus on receiving.

The final step is selling the play and timing. The biggest factor in selling the play is to draw no attention. Make the defense forget you're even on base. Take a safe lead on the pitches leading up to the delayed steal followed by a quiet secondary lead.

Timing the break can vary slightly, but typically, shuffle into your secondary, and as you land on the second hop, break for second base. The exact timing is determined by the pace of the pitcher's delivery. If he's quick to the plate, the runner breaks slightly earlier; if he's slow to the plate, the runner breaks later. You should break when the ball is about halfway to home plate.

7. Take advantage of breaking pitches in the dirt.

The pitcher has a 0-1 count on the hitter. He throws a breaking ball in the dirt, which the batter lays off and the catcher blocks. The runner on first base slides into second base uncontested.

Was it a delayed steal? No, the runner read the trajectory of the pitch and immediately broke for second.

In many cases, pitchers are throwing the breaking ball as a swing-and-miss pitch. They target the hitter's knees so that he commits to his swing before the ball breaks down and out of the strike zone. This pitching approach often results in the ball bouncing in the dirt. The catcher is taught to drop to his knees to block the pitch. From his knees, the catcher is attempting to *block* the pitch, not *catch* it. This provides an opening for the base runner to advance.

(Because they travel with top- and sidespin, breaking pitches bounce up and to the side. Fastballs and changeups have backspin, so it's a true, predictable bounce in the dirt that the catcher can pick. That is why the base runner has a better chance on a breaking ball in the dirt rather than a fastball or changeup.)

To execute this, runners need to anticipate the pitch. Pay attention to the count and the pitcher's patterns. We do it at the plate, so why not on the base paths? On base, the runner may also detect the pitcher's grip or catcher's sign that indicates a breaking pitch is about to be thrown. If the runner senses breaking pitch, he should focus on the trajectory of the pitch out of the pitcher's hand and get an aggressive secondary lead. If the ball is destined for the dirt, take off.

The chances of making it to second base are benefited twofold. First, because the catcher has dropped to his knees and blocked

The catcher is taught to drop to his knees on a ball in the dirt. As soon as you know from the trajectory of the pitch that it will bounce, take off.

the ball, he'll have little chance of making a throw. Second, if the catcher gloves the ball clean and quickly gets to a throwing position, the middle infielders may not react in time to cover the base. It almost serves like a delayed steal.

The beauty of this heads-up play is that if it's pulled off more than once, the pitcher will take notice. He'll think twice about bouncing a breaking ball, and then he becomes prone to leaving pitches up in the zone. That works to the advantage of the hitter.

8. Tag up on all foul balls.

With a runner on third and one out, the batter skies a pop-up in foul territory down the first-base line. The second baseman calls for the ball and makes a great over-the-shoulder catch. The runner from third scores standing up and the hitter chalks up a sacrifice fly.

Did the runner possess blazing speed? No. He simply took advantage of a quality defensive play.

Any time the ball is hit in the air in foul territory, go back to the base to tag. You may as well. There is nothing else for you to do on a foul ball. Defensive players become so focused on making what can be a difficult catch, they sometimes fail to pay any attention to the runners on base.

Pay special attention if an infielder is making a catch on the run on a foul ball that takes him away from the infield. A second baseman making a running catch in short right-field foul territory is a perfect time to tag from second base and advance to third. If the defensive player leaves his feet (dives or slides), the runner has an especially good chance of tagging up successfully. Also, be alert on a foul pop to the catcher when the backstop is deep behind home plate or if it takes him up the line. Tagging from first or second is a possibility, and if the pitcher fails to get off the mound and cover home, you can also tag from third and score.

Don't become a spectator on foul balls. A great catch can shift the momentum of a game. Immediately countering that, especially by tagging up, takes the wind out of the opponent's sails.

9. Take an extended one-way lead against a left-handed pitcher before stealing second.

A runner on first base takes a large lead. The pitcher senses he may attempt a steal and throws over to first. The runner gets back safely and then shortens his lead significantly. The pitcher lifts his leg and the runner takes off for second.

Does the runner have any chance to make it safely? Yes. Although he shortened his lead, he was able to break on first move from the pitcher.

Getting out to a big lead draws the attention of the pitcher. It begs him to throw over to first. Position yourself in a one-way lead, meaning your weight is on your left leg until you see the ball thrown to home plate. Then you bounce off into your secondary lead. However, the pitcher will likely throw over to first when he notices a substantial lead.

Prior to the ensuing pitch, take a lead approximately two-thirds the distance of where you were previously. This gives the pitcher a false sense of security. He sees that you've shortened up and pose less of a threat. The pitcher will likely deliver his next pitch to home plate. Now is when you're taking your educated risk and break on first move. This means as soon as the pitcher lifts his leg, you take off. Breaking on first move against a left-hander gives you a phenomenal jump. The catcher will have a very difficult time throwing you out.

Pitchers decide before they lift their leg whether they're going to first or throwing home. They do not adjust based on whether the runner breaks or not. If they tried, they'd balk almost every time. Set him up with a large, one-way lead and then take that calculated risk on the next pitch.

10. When you get picked off, don't stop—continue to second base.

With a left-handed pitcher on the mound, the runner on first base breaks for second as soon as the pitcher lifts his leg. The pitcher throws over to first and has him picked off. The runner never breaks stride and slides safely into second base.

Where did the defense go wrong? The answer lies in what the base runner did right.

With a left-handed pitcher on the mound, get into the habit of breaking on first move (as soon as the pitcher lifts his leg) when stealing second base. It's a heightened risk, but it provides the best shot for you to swipe second. Waiting until the left-handed pitcher's stride leg presses toward home plate takes too long.

Obviously, with risk comes failure, but you haven't necessarily failed if you break first move and the pitcher throws over to first. You're picked off, but you're not out yet.

When you break and the pitcher throws over to first, don't hesitate. Continue sprinting to second base. Do *not* get into a rundown. The only alteration is to adjust your path and run inside the baseline. This makes the throw and catch very difficult for the first baseman and shortstop. Think about it. The first baseman will step forward to receive the ball from the pitcher. The shortstop breaks to the inside of the base. By running in that throwing lane, you can cause problems with the flight of the throw and also the shortstop's view of the throw. This is an extremely tough and troublesome play for the defense to execute.

When taking your slide, target the outside of the base. Because the shortstop will be positioned to take the throw inside the base bag, sliding to the outside may help evade the tag.

If you're picked off first base, take an inside route to second base. This places you in the throwing lane of the first baseman, making the throw very difficult. Slide to the outside of second base.

Very fast runners sometimes slide safely into second purely based on speed. Any hesitation by the first baseman or a wide or high throw can provide just enough of a window to allow the runner to beat the throw. But even average runners can make it to second by never hesitating and crowding the throwing lane. Don't stop and get in a rundown. You're doing the defense a favor. Run inside the base and make them earn the out.

11. Use the slide to every possible advantage.

The batter hits a line-drive base hit to right-center field. He notices the outfielder take a poor route to the ball and he attempts to stretch into a double. The outfielder fields the ball clean and fires a strong throw that barely beats the runner. The shortstop applies the tag and the umpire calls the runner safe.

How was the runner safe? It sounds like he used his slide to avoid being tagged out.

Players slide into a base on close plays because it allows them to run as fast as they can for as long as possible. Going into a base standing up forces the player to slow down or risk overrunning the base. Sliding also makes applying a tag more difficult for the defensive player. Great base runners take that difficulty to its limits. Willie Mays is the best example of a player who possessed every slide imaginable to elude tags.

There is no rule that states you have to slide directly into a base. Your focus approaching the base, as a competitor, should be calculating which part of the base gives the best chance of sliding in safe. As manager Tony LaRussa once said, "The most aggressive thing in baseball is guys on base running around and sliding, raising dust."

Listed are some scenarios that good base runners look for when deciding how they're going to slide.

- On a very close force play (with a chance to beat the throw), slide directly into the base.
- On a force play where the lead runner is a sure out, slide aggressively toward the defensive player, but make sure you're within reach of the bag. Here you're sliding to make your teammate safe.
- If the runner is barely going to beat the throw on a tag play, slide directly into the base.
- If the infielder is receiving a high throw, slide directly into the base.
- If the infielder is receiving the ball on the outside of the base, slide to the inside of the base and vice versa.

- If the infielder is picking a short hop out of the dirt from the catcher, slide to the outside of the base.
- If the infielder is receiving an in-between hop, slide to the side of the base on which he is positioned. (He will have to shift his weight to his back leg to catch the ball cleanly.)
- If the throw beats the runner by a fair amount, slide past the base on the side opposite of where the defensive player is positioned. Catch the base with the foot (hook slide) or near-side hand, or turn back over and reach with the far-side arm. Defensive players are taught to apply the tag, quickly get out, and show the umpire the ball. If the runner avoids the tag, the defensive player is often out of position and off-balance to apply a second tag. The bottom line is, if you're dead on the play, try something creative to get there safely.

Remember, when you slide, try to be safe! Slide so that the fielder has the most difficult tag possible. It's your last-ditch effort to keep your mission of scoring a run alive.

12. Assuming can make you look dumb; anticipating will make you look good.

On a routine single up the middle, the ball takes a bad hop on the center fielder, hits off his shoulder, and caroms 20 feet away. The batter who assumes the fielder catches the ball remains at first. The batter who anticipates a botched play ends up at second.

Which would you like to be?

Coaches tell players to never assume anything on the baseball field. And for the most part they're correct. There are no guarantees in baseball. Assuming the defense will make every play can make you look foolish. But what if you didn't assume, but rather anticipated. And instead of anticipating clean execution, you anticipated a mistake? That would always put you in a position to take the extra base if a mishap occurs and may even cause a few mistakes by constantly applying pressure.

As Branch Rickey once explained, "Take that extra base every time. Make them throw after you; make them hurry their throws. You'll get thrown out for sure, but for every time they throw you out now, you will make them hurry and throw wild later. You will reap a golden harvest of extra bases."

It's like a goal scorer in soccer. The player anticipates a bad trap or a miskick by a defensive back on every play. He may be wrong the entire game until the back makes that one subtle error and he's right there to pounce on the loose ball and take it in for a scoring chance. Infielders and outfielders back each other up because they realize that mistakes happen. Base runners should behave similarly.

Poor judgment, technique, and field conditions all contribute to routine plays turning into opportunities to advance an extra base. If you anticipate the mistake, you're a heads-up ballplayer who hustles. If you assume no mistake will be made, you risk embarrassment and appear lazy and disinterested.

13. Look to steal third on the throwback from the catcher.

With one out and a mediocre runner on second base, the catcher receives the pitch, remains in his squat position, and tosses the ball back to the pitcher. As the ball is released, the runner breaks for third and slides in safely.

Can third base be stolen on the catcher? In this case, it was.

Base coaches will tell you that third base is stolen on the pitcher more often than on the catcher. In most cases that is correct on a straight steal. However, when a player notices a catcher throwing the ball back without pace on an arc, never getting out of squat position, and/or generally being lethargic behind the plate, the stage is set to steal third on the throwback.

This is a gutsy play that entails thorough investigation. You'll have a better chance of pulling this off if you've observed this behavior from the catcher before reaching second base. That way, you can immediately work on getting a larger secondary lead and timing the play without drawing attention. Recognizing this after reaching second base may not give you enough pitches to execute the play.

Break into a quiet secondary lead to give a sense of calm. You want to act casual and harmless. Don't appear runnerish. Stay relaxed with all of your movements.

On the pitch on which you've decided to steal, time your movements along with the catcher's. Take a delayed secondary lead so that you maintain some momentum toward third base. As the catcher

An inattentive, lazy catcher can be exploited. As his arm swings upward, break.

begins to move his arm forward to the point of release, take off for third.

A couple of factors will help make this play less of a risk. A right-handed pitcher has a tougher throw on this play once he receives the return throw from the catcher. He has to open his body to the right, which often causes errant throws. (Left-handers have an easier throw.) Also, if the third baseman is playing deep, it makes the base easier to steal. He'll have trouble getting to the base in time to receive the throw and apply a tag.

14. First and third with a left-hander on the mound is an opportunity to steal home.

With runners on first and third and a left-hander on the mound, the runner on third breaks and steals home.

Legs or brains? A little bit of both.

The first-and-third situation is one that teams practice defending. Hours are spent on first-and-third defenses. The runner on first attempts to steal second to draw the throw from the catcher, allowing the runner on third to break for home. Only perfect execution by the defense will enable them to cut the runner down at the plate.

With a left-hander on the mound, however, you can steal home on your own or be assisted by the runner at first.

You may remember Aaron Hill of the Toronto Blue Jays stealing home on Andy Pettitte of the New York Yankees in May 2007. Pettitte took the sign, and as he moved to the set position, Hill broke from third base. Pettitte was facing first base and couldn't see Hill at third. Yankees catcher Jorge Posada jumped out and yelled for Pettitte to throw home. Pettitte stepped off the rubber with his left foot and fired home. Too late. Hill scored on a great baserunning play.

Hill indicated that timing is essential in executing this successfully. But he also mentioned that despite being nervous, there are times you just have to go for it.

"He's looking forward and right when he starts to bring his hands up and looks at first base; that's really the only time you can go," said Hill. "I definitely felt my heart beating. That's for sure. I just pictured the umpire calling me safe and hoped that'd give me a little extra boost."

The play was the difference in a 3–2 win for the Blue Jays. The opportunity presented itself and Hill possessed the knowledge and courage to pull it off. It was an example of a base runner using the sixth tool to do something unusual.

A second way to pull this play off is to be in cahoots with the runner on first base. The runner at first takes an extended, one-way lead and draws the throw from the left-handed pitcher. As soon as the pitcher lifts his leg to throw over to first base, break for home. The first baseman has to await the throw, receive it, and throw home. A swift runner can score easily on this play if it's timed right.

In 1986, Mike Schmidt and Glen Wilson pulled off a steal of home to win a game for the Philadelphia Phillies against the New York Mets. Wilson was on first base and faked tripping over his feet and falling down. The alert pitcher threw to first base and Schmidt raced from third and crossed home plate easily. That is a prime example of using imagination and taking a risk.

15.   Look to take two bases on a sacrifice bunt.

With a runner on first and nobody out, the batter squares to bunt. The ball is bunted to third base and the runner is thrown out at first. The runner at first advances all the way to third base.

Is this a set play? It can be if the defense helps set the table.

With a runner on first base in a sacrifice bunt situation, the batter should bunt toward first and force the first baseman to field the ball. Because he's holding the runner on, he can't charge as early as the third baseman. Making the first baseman field the ball gives the runner the best chance of advancing to second base.

Sometimes, the ball is bunted to third base. If this is the case, pay attention to how the third baseman reacts after throwing the ball to first. If he doesn't retreat, third base may be left vacant.

In this situation, the second baseman is shifting to cover first base and the shortstop is covering second base in hopes of forcing out the lead runner. The third baseman has to leave third base unoccupied to move in and field the bunt. Third basemen are taught to throw the ball and retreat to the bag, but often they're caught spectating. The runner advancing to second (assuming the play goes to first) should round second and continue to third base.

Commonly, this play becomes a footrace to third between the base runner and the shortstop or the third baseman. Throwing the ball across the diamond to an unoccupied base is a risky play for the first baseman, and he'll often tuck the ball into his glove. After all, if the ball is thrown away at third base, the runner can score, and throwing to a moving target is very discomforting.

Taking two bases is also a possibility with a runner on second. If the catcher vacates home plate to make a play, look to take advantage as the base runner. The combination of your aggressiveness and the element of surprise may enable you to score on the play.

16.   Draw the snap throw from the catcher to steal third.

A runner at second base is taking a big secondary lead and taking his time retreating to second on the pitch. The catcher notices the runner is in no-man's-land and, on the ensuing pitch, receives the ball and fires a throw to second. The runner coasts into third base.

Did the runner dodge a bullet on the pickoff throw? It's more like he loaded the gun and placed the catcher's finger on the trigger.

Baseball Etiquette: When to Shut Down the Running Game

If your team is blowing out the opponent, the etiquette of the game calls for you to shut down the running game. That means no more stealing. It's a display of poor sportsmanship.

The question is how big of a lead warrants the "no steal" sign? The number ranges from six to eight runs. The coach needs to consider several factors that determine precisely when to stop running, such as how far along you are in the game, the talent level of your team and the opposing team (that is, are they likely to come back), the size of the field, and so forth. The bottom line is coaches should practice common sense and have a feel for whether or not the game is out of reach.

It is OK to advance on passed balls and wild pitches (with the exception of a runner on third base), but there should not be steal signs, hit-and-run plays, or bunts when the game is out of reach. Teams should also keep in mind that if they stop running and the opponent comes back, they can always reinstate the running game.

Joe Gmitter was an All-American shortstop at Rider University. He was a five-tool player, but his use of the sixth tool made him exceptional. Joe used this play to swipe third base time and time again.

Joe was fast and courageous on the bases, but an essential component to his makeup was how nonchalant he *seemed* on the base paths. His stat line provided evidence of a base stealer, but after watching him through a few pitches, he made you forget all about what his numbers indicated. It's as if he were in a poker game and was dealt a feeble hand. That was Joe's poker face.

At second base, Joe would bounce off into a healthy secondary lead and casually get back to the base. He gave off a vibe that he wasn't really paying attention after the pitch, that his mind was elsewhere. While the catcher thought he was picking up on something he could exploit, he was actually being reeled in by Joe. By the third or fourth pitch, the catcher had signaled to a middle infielder to cover second after the pitch. He'd rifle a throw to second to pick Joe, but Joe was gone. He immediately took off for third when he saw the catcher pop out of his stance and draw his arm back.

The cool thing about this play was that it showcased two players using their sixth tool. Joe's tool simply had a sharper point as he was one step ahead of his opponent.

17. Look in when stealing second.

A runner takes off for second base on the pitch. The ball is hit on the ground to first base. The second baseman points to the sky and looks up. The runner puts on the brakes and begins to retreat back to first base. He is eventually tagged out on the play.

Why was the runner so confused? He failed to glance in at home plate on the steal.

Never assume the batter will take the pitch when stealing. Instead, glance in to see if the batter hits the ball and, if so, where. You should be able to sense when the pitch is entering the hitting zone and turn your head inward to witness if the ball is struck. This will assist you in deciding whether you should slide into second, stay up and continue to third base, stop at second and pick up the play, or retreat to first base immediately.

When stealing, glance in to see if the hitter swings. If he hits the ball in the air, you may have to retreat.

On a straight steal, you're focused on an explosive jump and getting from point A to point B as quickly as possible. The best-case scenario is if the hitter takes or swings through a pitch. When he swings and makes contact, however, you need to quickly react to the result. This can help you advance extra bases or avoid being doubled up.

A quick note: this advice goes double on hit-and-run plays. The runner(s) *must* look in because the batter is definitely swinging to protect the runner.

18. Don't make the last out of an inning at third base.

With a runner on first and two outs, the hitter slaps a base hit to right field. The base runner takes a risk going first to third, and he's thrown out at third.

Is this a situation in which the third-base coach pats his player on the shoulder for being aggressive? No, this was not a smart risk, and the player needs to be addressed after the game.

Making the final out at third base is a mental mistake. If you're at second base, you're already in scoring position. A hit can score you from second. There is no need to risk getting thrown out at third, whether it be off a hit, a ball in the dirt, or a straight steal.

Is there a better chance of scoring from third base than second base? Absolutely. It's one step away from home plate. Taking a risk getting there is only sensible, however, if there is one or no outs. If there is no risk, meaning you're 100 percent sure you'll get there safely, then by all means take the base. If there is risk, however, don't do it. It's a boneheaded baserunning blunder when you end the inning at third base.

19. A runner can produce a better time in the 100-meter dash if he starts from 95 meters away.

A base runner attempts to steal second and is thrown out by a hair.

Can this be attributed to the catcher's arm strength, the pitcher's quick delivery, or the speed of the runner? Perhaps it's one of these reasons or a combination of several. The length of the lead, however, could also be the difference.

Generally speaking, base runners do not get enough of a lead. It goes back to the fear factor. The thought of being picked off looms so large that runners get too conservative. Understand the purpose

Good base runners dive back into bases when pitchers throw over. If you can get back standing up, you can get more. This goes for fast and slow runners.

of a lead, though. It's to get closer to the next base. Every inch closer provides the runner a better chance of sliding in safe on a steal or force play or advancing on a pitch in the dirt.

New York Mets shortstop Jose Reyes has exceptional running speed. No one can argue that his ability to steal bases is primarily because of his quickness. But Reyes deserves credit for the size of his leads as well. Have you ever watched how many times he nearly gets picked off in a game? It's frightening for Mets fans watching, but Reyes is able to steal so many bags partially because of the boldness of his leads. He enhances his odds of being safe before even taking his first step.

Get off first base and push the envelope. If the pitcher throws over and you can get back safely standing up, that means you can get more. Take an additional step and get back to the base on your belly if he throws over.

If you've gone through a number of games without nearly getting picked off, your lead isn't big enough. Get out some more and make the pitcher think about you. It's a distraction that diminishes his focus on the hitter.

While on the subject of getting a more aggressive lead, look to the list below for a few don'ts when taking a lead off first base.

- Never let your eyes leave the pitcher. Don't look back to the base to see how far you are. Count your steps so you have a frame of reference. If your eyes leave the pitcher and he throws over, you're out.
- Don't cross your feet. If you take a crossover step (left over right) when getting out to a lead, you can get tangled up when trying to get back. A savvy pitcher will time it just right to nail you.
- Stay grounded. In other words, don't hop out to a lead. Again, a crafty pitcher will take notice of this. Once you leave your feet, he'll turn and fire. You will have to wait until your right foot lands before being able to change direction and get back. Slide your feet along the ground when getting out to a lead; don't hop.

20. When on second base, look to score on a ground ball to the infield.

With a runner on second base, a ground ball is hit toward the middle. It's to the runner's left, so he takes off for third base. The shortstop makes a great play, throws to first, but the runner is safe. Before the defense can argue, the runner from second base crosses home plate.

How did he score? He never stopped.

Any time you're on second base and a ground ball is hit at you or to your left, think about trying to score. The throw is going to first base, so as you approach third, you can take a small turn. The job of the third-base coach is to get down the third-base line to stop you. If he doesn't stop you, you're scoring. Here's what can happen to enable you to score that you can't see until it's too late to take advantage of, unless you take the turn:

- The ball gets past the infielder and rolls into the outfield.
- The ball is thrown past the first baseman.
- The ball is thrown in the dirt and the first baseman fails to pick it clean. (It gets away from him.)
- The ball is thrown late to first base and the third-base coach feels the runner from second can score. (This takes speed from the base runner, a good jump, and no hesitation.)
- The third-base coach has a hunch that the first baseman will be caught off guard and deliver a late throw to home plate.

As the runner, also be aggressive on a slow roller or chopper to the shortstop or third baseman. Because they have to come in on the ball, you can advance to third base even though the ball is to your right. This type of ball often produces late throws to first base. You might be able to score on the play. The same idea goes when the hitter bunts for a base hit.

21. If you have the open hand on first base, try to see the catcher's signs to the pitcher.

The runner on first has the green light to steal at any time. The first pitch is a fastball. He doesn't go. The second pitch is a fastball; he doesn't go. The third pitch is a breaking ball; he goes.

How did he know to go on the third pitch? He either had a feeling or saw the catcher's sign.

Good base stealers are sometimes given the open hand from the third-base coach—that means they are permitted to steal whenever they want. The best pitch to steal on is something off-speed.

When taking your lead, glance in toward the catcher to see if you can pick up his signs. Don't turn your head toward him or you'll give yourself away. Just shift your eyes. If you pick the time that he

When taking your lead at first base, shift your eyes in toward the catcher intermittently to try to pick up signs. Multiple fingers means it's a good time to go.

Picking up the catcher's signs can help you
steal third or alert the hitter to what pitch is
coming.

is giving signs, he has the pitcher's attention, which allows your eyes
to leave the pitcher and take a peek.

What you're looking for is one finger or multiple fingers. That's it.
If you see multiple fingers, it's a good time to go. Whether it's a curveball, slider, changeup, or splitter, it's something off-speed. The pitch
takes longer to get to the catcher and is typically thrown down. Low
pitches increase the release time for the catcher because he has a longer
distance to transfer the ball from receiving it to the point of release.

If the catcher shields his fingers from your sight, it doesn't mean
you're relegated to rolling the dice. Pick a pitch that you feel will be
off-speed. Think as though you're the hitter. If you sense a breaking
ball is about to be thrown, get a good lead and take off.

22. Look in at the catcher's signals when occupying second base.

*With a runner on second base and the count 1-1, the pitcher throws a
slider that breaks away from the hitter. The hitter stays on it and drills
it to the opposite-field gap for a run-scoring double.*

*Did the hitter guess slider? He may have, or he may have been told
what was coming.*

When standing on second base, you have a full view of the catcher's signs. Inexperienced catchers will give a single sign to the pitcher. If you're witness to a catcher who doesn't go through a series of signs, tell the hitter what pitch is coming. A simple visual sign can be "hands on my knees—fastball, hands off my knees—off-speed." Don't make the sign obvious like holding fingers up because someone on the defense will notice and make the adjustment.

Catchers who go through a series of signs will also make the mistake of giving the live pitch only once in the series. In other words, they put down four signs and only put down the number one a single time. The number one was the second sign given. When the pitcher throws a fastball, you now know it's the second sign. Another example of a series, one-one-two-one-four. The pitcher throws a curveball. The pitch is the third sign.

Use this information also when you're looking to steal third base. A breaking ball from a right-handed pitcher thrown to a right-handed batter makes it a tougher throw for the catcher. Pick a curveball, try to get a walking lead, and take off.

23. Read the pitcher when attempting to steal second.

A runner is on first base and has the steal sign. A right-handed pitcher is on the mound and is set. Just before he lifts up his foot, the base runner takes off.

How did he know to leave early? The pitcher has a "tell" before he delivers.

When attempting to steal second base off a right-handed pitcher, you typically look at the pitcher's feet. Once his left foot lifts upward, you take off. There are some pitchers, however, who give away delivery home before that left foot picks up.

Pitchers who have their weight evenly distributed or slightly forward in the set position will sometimes lean or rock back before lifting their left foot. You'll notice their lower body load back or their entire body rock back to initiate their motion. If you see this, take off immediately. They can't rock back and then throw over. It's a balk.

Another common "tell" is their left shoulder will turn inward to start their delivery. Once their shoulder turns in, they must deliver the ball to home plate or, again, it's a balk. Watch the front shoulder and if it's active early, break.

Some pitchers set their hands high when throwing over and let them relax at the waist when delivering to the plate.

Pitchers also get into habits when they are throwing over. Where they hold their hands in the set position is often an indication. If his hands (and glove) are held high around the chest, he's coming over. If they rest down by his belt, he's going home. The width of his feet in the set position, pattern of looks over (or nods), and posture can also indicate whether he's throwing to first or home. Watch from the dugout as a team and you're likely to discover something.

24. Draw a throw to first from the pitcher early in the game.

The leadoff hitter hits a base hit up the middle to start the game. The runner gets out to a very big lead, and the pitcher throws over. The runner gets back safely.

Does this have any significance? Yes, the base runner is doing his job of getting the pitcher to show his move.

Early in the game, force the pitcher to show his move. Whether he's right-handed or left-handed, it's important to see the quality of his move to first. That will determine the length of your team's leads at first base for the game. Once you get on base (especially if you're the first runner to reach base), it's your responsibility to make him throw to first. Employ a one-way lead in this situation.

Looking Bad by Not Looking

During the 2007 season, Philadelphia Phillies outfielder Michael Bourn stole second base in the bottom of the ninth inning of a game against the Arizona Diamondbacks. The Phillies trailed 4–3 and Bourn put himself in scoring position with one out.

Ryan Howard, the 2006 National League MVP, came up to the plate. The Diamondbacks shifted their defense, putting the shortstop on the second-base side and the second baseman in short right field. Howard roped a line drive to right field and Bourn immediately broke for third base. The ball was caught by D-backs second baseman Orlando Hudson, who promptly threw the ball to second base for the game-ending double play.

Checking the infield and outfield defense can allow you to both anticipate and look good. In this case, Bourn looked bad by not checking the defensive alignment.

If the pitcher is smart, he won't show you his best move right away. He'll casually throw over to keep you honest. If this is the case, get out a little more and force him to speed up his pickoff move. Don't get too crazy because, remember, you haven't seen his best yet. But challenge him to show your teammates whether he's quick to first or not.

It's better to be on the safe side with a left-handed pitcher. Get out to a one-way lead and try to get his best move. If he doesn't show it, continue to use a one-way lead, but make certain he delivers the pitch home before shuffling into your secondary lead. If he has a really good lefty move, you may be his first victim of the day if you don't see him throw home.

25. Draw throws from the outfielders whenever possible.

A shallow fly ball is hit to the outfield. The right fielder catches the ball and fires home to nail the runner tagging.

Should the runner tag on this play? At the very least, he should fake a tag.

Anytime you can, draw a throw from the defense. The excitement of the play may cause an errant throw and allow you to advance. It can also help a teammate who is two bases behind you to advance.

A great time to draw a throw is during a first-and-third situation with one out. On a short fly ball to left field, the left fielder is hoping you'll tag. He knows he has a good chance to get an outfield assist. You (on third base) are in his line of vision to home plate. If he sees you on the base and notices you break hard as he catches the ball, he's uncorking a throw.

Two good things can happen out of this. One, he throws the ball wild and off target or sails the throw over the catcher's head. You can now score on the play. Two, if he throws the ball all the way home on a line, a heads-up runner on first base can tag and advance to second base. Now you have two runners in scoring position.

Draw a throw from outfield (or infield) whenever possible. There is no risk, but there's a possible reward.

3
Defense

This chapter is titled "Defense," but a sixth-tool player still thinks offensively when wearing his glove. He doesn't simply wait for the ball to be hit to him to secure an out. He pursues outs. He uses his imagination to create out opportunities. A great defensive player counters the traditional thinker on the base paths by fostering original thoughts. Remember, you spend a lot more time with your glove than with a bat.

To play good defense, you first have to be prideful. You have to care about your defensive performance and how important it is to being a good baseball player. If you consider yourself an excellent hitter and an adequate fielder, that's all you'll ever be on the defense. You've got to bring the same enthusiasm out onto the field as you do to the plate and on the base paths. Search for runners making big turns. Take the initiative to run a pick play on the trail runner. Observe the field conditions to perfect your positioning, and watch the base coaches and opposing players in an attempt to pick up signs. Don't be reactive on the field. Be proactive.

"Don't get me wrong, I Iike to hit," said Willie Mays. "But there's nothing like getting out there in the outfield, running after a ball, and throwing somebody out trying to take that extra base. That's real fun."

To play the defensive game you must anticipate and communicate. Anticipation prepares you for what's coming so you can execute properly, but it also allows you to think ahead to your next move. Your thinking can't be limited to what you'll do with the ball when it's hit to you and where you should be when it's not hit to you. It must be broader. You must think about the base runners and their actions. What do they see? Where is their attention? When will they be looking to take an extra base? Walking a mile in the shoes of a base runner brings to light opportunities to slay them along the way.

Communication is so important on defense because many instinctive plays require a collective effort from your teammates. It is fruitless to recognize a perfect chance for a snap throw to first base from the catcher if you don't have the attention and understanding from the catcher. Practice is the best time to work on communication with teammates. Review scenarios, exchange signals, and discuss set plays so they can be practiced. When plays are practiced, the timing and execution improves along with your confidence. It is then you will be more willing to take that calculated risk in the game.

You can also communicate between innings. Sharing information with teammates forces them to become more observant during a game. If they're not being attentive on the field now, they will be when there's a threat of letting down their teammates. When discussions about out opportunities begin occurring on a regular basis, it becomes a source of pride and a part of your team's identity. Thoughts will evolve into, "You better pay attention on the bases against us. If not, we'll make you pay." Now you've got yourself a solid and dangerous defensive unit.

Each team gets only 27 outs in a nine-inning game. There is no way for the opposition to attain additional outs. Those 27 are all they get. The more outs you can take away from them, the better chance your team has to win. Chew up their outs as quickly as possible so you can get off the field and hit. No team has ever taken a lead while standing in the field.

Tips for Playing Great Defense

The following tips teach defensive players to be active, aggressive, and offensive-minded. Playing great defense entails more than making routine plays. It requires an opportunistic approach from a player who is smart and confident.

Aggressively pursuing outs will make you a better defensive player and a valuable asset to your team.

1. The best fielding practice occurs during batting practice.

A left fielder has taken fly ball after fly ball from his coach in practice. Balls that start at him eventually fade to his left.

In the game, the fly ball is hit directly to the left fielder, but this time the ball fades to his right. He makes the catch, but nearly misjudged the ball.

What happened? Balls hit off a fungo bat are different from balls hit live.

Positioning, range, and technique are very important to playing solid defense, but judging balls off the bat is also essential. To improve your judgment reading balls off the bat, field balls at your position during batting practice. This simulates precisely how balls will come off the bat in games. As Tony LaRussa explains, "You can take 1,000 fungoes a day and it won't be as good as 10 minutes pretending you're in a game, taking balls off the bat during batting practice."

Taking ground balls off a fungo bat from a coach does have value, but you'll fail to encounter different types of ground balls. Topspin ground balls, for example, shoot or take a charged hop on the second bounce. Balls off an inside-out swing will run away from you. Cue shots off the very end of the bat will catch the grass and kick depending on the direction of the spin. Most of the ground balls you field from fungo bats are hit pure and at the same pace.

Fly balls react very differently when comparing live batted balls to fungoes. In left field, for example, everything hit off a bat hooks (right-handed hitter) or fades (left-handed hitter) toward the foul line if it's not hit square on the nose. You will not see this from a ball hit off a fungo bat. Balls will be hit true (straight) or fade (slice). Fly balls off a fungo will rarely draw (or hook). So your practice habits can actually cause you to misjudge a ball in the game if you're not careful.

Taking balls live off the bat also improves your jumps. You'll get better at recognizing the timing of the swing and pitch and the angle at which the ball comes off the bat. You'll find yourself moving to the ball before it's hit. Your ability to determine whether a ball is hit off the barrel, below the barrel (jammed), or above the barrel (off the end) will also improve so that your reaction time is better in deciding whether to come in, go back, or stay put.

Batting practice is often treated as a time to stand around and talk. Instead, use this time to your advantage. Go to your primary position and field everything hit in your area. After sufficient practice time, move to your secondary position and even a third position to get reads from a different spot on the field. You never know when you may be asked to play a new position.

2. Know thyself in the field.

A third baseman is playing very deep with a runner on second and two outs. A ground ball is hit to his left. He fields it and rifles a throw to first base for an out.

Why was he playing so deep? Considering the situation, he wants to play as deep as his arm strength allows him to play.

Much the way hitters and pitchers must acknowledge their strengths and weaknesses, you must do the same in the field. Arm strength, speed, quickness, and lateral mobility must be taken into account when setting up to play defense.

What type of player are you? Do you move well but only have an adequate arm? Do you possess phenomenal arm strength but lack mobility? Whatever the case, consider what you do well and not so well in the field and play your position accordingly.

Let's say you're a center fielder who has below-average arm strength. It's likely that you run well or you wouldn't be out there. With runners on base, you may have to shorten your outfield depth. Work on getting really good at coming to the ball quickly, minimizing your steps, and having a quick release. Getting to and rid of the ball rapidly can make up for a lesser throwing arm.

Another example is if you play third base and have a great arm but slow feet. Play deeper to give yourself more time to react and move to the ball. Although you'll get the ball a little later and the throw will be longer, the strength of your throw will make up time.

Factor your strengths and weaknesses into your game play, but isolate the weaknesses to work on in practice. Don't avoid your shortcomings because they will eventually limit your playing time or opportunities to advance.

3. Always want and expect the ball to be hit to you.

A humpback line drive is hit to center field. The center fielder is sprinting at the ball immediately and makes a sliding catch.

How did he get such a good jump? He wanted the ball and expected it on every pitch.

Proper positioning can be the difference between an out and a clean single. Consider your arm strength, foot speed, and speed of the runner when assuming your ready position.

How many times have you seen this play, but instead the ball drops in front of the center fielder for a base hit? It drives the pitcher crazy. That center fielder may have physical ability, but he's either in la-la land or fearful of making a mistake. He'd rather play it safe.

As a defensive player, you've got to have an offensive mind-set. Your body language is so important in the field because it prepares you to make plays. Stay positive with your body language and look alert. It readies you mentally and physically for what's coming. Pride yourself on being an athlete on every pitch.

Bad body language from defensive players is easy to pick out. They're more upright, they move slowly, and they appear tentative. They're also not talking and seem disinterested. They're either not expecting the ball or are hoping the ball is hit elsewhere. Guess what? It's coming.

Look forward to the difficult plays. They provide you with an opportunity to shine, to make the exceptional play. Hot shots, backhands, slow rollers, or balls driven deep to the outfield gap are chances to excel and bail out your pitcher. Receiving bad throws at a base gives you a chance to make a great play and bail out a teammate. Relish those plays rather than shying away from them.

When you're playing defense, consider your position as your personal area on the field. And like a hockey goaltender does with his net, don't let anything infiltrate your area. Any ball that is hit near you will be captured. Nothing will be permitted to pass by.

4. Show off your arm during pregame warm-ups and between innings.

During infield/outfield practice, the center fielder throws at half speed to the cutoff man. He's saving his arm for the game.

Is this smart? No, it isn't. He's guaranteeing he'll have to use his arm in the game.

Players sometimes think they're being sly by not showing their true arm strength during pregame warm-ups or between innings. The thinking is, "I'll let them think I have a weak arm, and when they go, I'll gun them down." But what you're really doing is giving the opponent cause to be aggressive on the bases. The best way to control an offense is to make them run the bases station to station.

This is especially important if you're an outfielder or catcher. Do you think Pudge Rodriguez is most valuable behind the plate because he throws out runners? No. His greatest value is that his presence behind the plate stops the running game before it starts. He stymies the run based on the opponents' knowledge of his strong arm. Great outfield arms like Vladimir Guerrero, Jeff Francoeur, and Shane Victorino force base coaches to put up the stop sign. When the runner doesn't even attempt to advance, that is an efficiency rate of 100 percent.

Dwight Evans was a great outfielder for the Boston Red Sox who had an exceptional throwing arm. Evans was a strong proponent of showcasing his talent before the game started. "A lot of times the other team watches you—especially the third-base coach—and they'll see what you're throwing, and it will stay in their head. You want to plant that seed. Let them think about it so when the game comes, the runner peeks at you as he's going, the third-base coach's arms somehow go up, stopping the runner. So you charge hard in practice and throw well—just as if it's in a game."

Let it loose during pregame. If you have a weaker outfield arm, play shallow during infield/outfield to shorten your throws and give the perception of a quality arm. Catchers should zip the ball around the bases and down to second each time between innings. It sends the message, "Don't even think about trying."

5. Play the game before the ball is pitched.

Runners are on first and second base with one out. A slow ground ball is hit to third base. The third baseman charges, fields on the move, and fires a strike to first base for the out.

How did he know to throw to first base? Because he reviewed this play before the ball was hit.

Coaches advise defensive players to relax in the field. That's when players perform at their very best. In order to relax, however, you've got to know what you're going to do with the ball before it is hit. To accomplish this, review the scenarios in your mind before the pitch is thrown. This will improve not only your execution but also your ability to anticipate on the field.

Every fielder should undertake this practice whether playing first base, pitcher, or right field. Here are a few general points to consider before addressing specific details.

- What is the score? Are you winning or losing and by how much?
- What inning is it?
- How many outs are there?

These points will determine whether you're conservative in the field (get the out), or aggressive (get the lead runner). From there, a number of elements come into play. How fast is the runner at bat? How fast are the runners on base? How fast are you? Do you have a strong arm or below-average arm strength? What are the field conditions? What will the other positions on the field do if the ball is hit to them? There is no shortage of information to review.

On balls hit to you with runners on base, what you do with the ball can depend on how and precisely where it is hit. Balls hit to your right, left, or directly at you can influence where the play is made. Also, the pace of the hit can determine the play.

Don't be self-absorbed when reviewing potential plays. Think about what you should or can do when a ball is hit to another teammate. Covering bases, backing up bases, or setting up at a base for a

With a comfortable lead late in the game, take
the sure out whenever in doubt.

follow-up play after the initial play is made can be critical. Anticipate
where the throw is going and how you can be involved. This is especially important in the outfield. With a runner on first and a ground
ball to the first baseman, for example, the throw is going to second
base for the force. If you're playing left field, back up the throw to
second base. This throw is tough to execute and sometimes ends up
in left-center field. If you anticipate the bad throw, the runner will be
unable to advance. If you're spectating, he'll take third easily.

The checklist of scenarios may seem endless, but the more you
do it, the easier it becomes. You'll develop your instincts. This is also
why it's helpful to play different positions. The more positions you
learn, the better you'll understand the game and the easier it will
become for you to anticipate what can go wrong on a given play and
how you can get involved to help keep things under control.

6. If you miss your target on defense, miss low.

*The right fielder charges a base hit and attempts to throw out the base
runner going from first to third base. His throw short-hops the third
baseman. The third baseman picks the ball and applies the tag to get
the runner.*

Keeping the ball down on throws to the base always gives the baseman a chance to glove the ball. Also, it puts his glove in good position to apply a tag.

Was this a bad throw? Not nearly as bad as it would have been if it was wild high.

In a perfect world, infielders and outfielders would be accurate with every throw they uncork. Unfortunately, that is unrealistic, but if the errant throws could miss low rather than high, there would be more outs and fewer bases advanced on overthrows.

Low throws give the fielder at the bag a chance. He could pick the ball clean, receive it on a bounce or in-between hop, or at the very least, block the ball. A throw that is too high is simply too high to reach. The baseman has no opportunity to make a play. Also, if the fielder does catch a high throw, it takes him longer to apply the tag.

High throws occur when the fielder is trying to put something extra on the throw. He tilts back and then opens his shoulders on the throw, causing the arm to drag behind and release the ball too high. When making a strong throw, think about keeping the fingers on top of the ball and throwing downhill. Convince yourself you have a strong enough arm; the throw just has to be on line and accurate.

With a play at home plate, throws that sail over the cutoff man's head are devastating to team defense. It will likely fail to get the runner at the plate, and when the other base runners see that the throw is too high for the cutoff man, they can advance. Instead of an RBI single and a runner on first, it's an RBI single with a runner in scoring position. Keep the ball down when throwing to give your teammates a chance.

7. With runners on first and second in a bunt situation, have the pitcher attempt an inside move to see if the hitter shows bunt.

The pitcher is set in the stretch with runners on first and second. He lifts his leg and turns toward second base but does not throw.

Is this a broken pickoff play? No, he's just trying to get the batter to show if the bunt is on.

Certain late-game situations call for a sacrifice bunt. There is no guarantee, however, and before a defense moves into bunt coverage, it's helpful to know if the batter is indeed bunting. The infield will be wide-open if he swings away.

Once the pitcher lifts his leg, the hitter will begin moving his feet and sliding his hands on the bat if he's bunting. You now have assurance of a bunt in the infield and can break into your bunt coverage more aggressively. The inside move also forces the runner at second to take a more conservative primary and secondary lead.

8. Keep the runner honest at second, but remember your responsibility to field your position.

The second baseman is holding a speedy runner close. He's only a few steps from the base, and the catcher is set up away to a right-handed hitter. The pitch is thrown and the batter hits a ground ball through the right side for a run-scoring single.

A good piece of hitting? Good hitting combined with poor infield positioning.

Your job in the middle infield with a runner on second base is to keep the runner *honest*. It's not to *hold* the runner on base. Shading too far toward the base leaves a large gap in the infield. You don't want to surrender a ground-ball base hit because you're too concerned with a runner's lead. Give the runner some attention, but don't allow it to cause poor infield positioning.

9. When taking throws on a force play at second base from the pitcher or catcher, go to the front of the base.

A ball is hit back to the pitcher, and he turns to second to start a potential double play. The pitcher throws the ball in the dirt, and the shortstop picks up the ball to get the force out.

Was the shortstop lucky? "Luck is the residue of design," said Branch Rickey. He was positioned to take the throw in front of the base.

Pitchers can throw strikes all day, but ask them to throw to a base and it's as if they're blindfolded. A common mistake is that pitchers tense up and hold on to the ball too long. This produces a low throw.

As the middle infielder, taking the throw in front of the base gives you the opportunity to pick up a low throw in the dirt. Standing behind the bag puts the bag into play. This also goes for taking a throw from the catcher.

The second reason for taking the throw in front is that you receive the ball sooner. The quicker you get it, the earlier you can get rid of it. This especially helps on throws from the catcher.

10. When cutting the ball off on a base hit to the outfield, look to throw behind the runner.

The leadoff batter drives a base hit to left-center field. The left fielder gloves the ball and throws it to the shortstop, who's out for the cutoff. The shortstop turns and fires a strike to the first baseman to nail the runner.

How did he know the runner would be off first base? He took advantage of the player's human nature.

When a player drives a base hit to the outfield, he is taught to make a turn. If the outfielder mishandles or arrives late to the ball, the runner is in position to continue to second base. Many players are guilty of what Dave Gallagher calls "false hustle." They circle the base hard, make a strong turn, then turn around and retreat to first base. These guys are prime targets for this play.

Go to the front of second base on throws from the pitcher and catcher when there is a force. Also, remember to tell the pitcher before the pitch that you're covering.

With a strong turn, they're a good 30 feet from first base. When they retreat, they turn their backs to the play. The runner often jogs back to the base, thinking of nothing but how happy he is with himself for getting a hit.

If you're playing shortstop on this play, be thinking from the get-go. A hit that is slightly away from the outfielder will encourage a more aggressive turn from the runner. Set yourself in a position to receive the cut that puts you in line with first base. In your mind, you are going to receive the throw from the outfielder, immediately turn, and fire to first base. As you turn, your eyes are looking at two things: is the first baseman in position, and is the runner far enough off the base to get him. If it's on, get him! Communication with the first baseman is key. Tell him to always be around the base on a sure base hit.

This is not isolated to shortstops or base hits. There are many opportunities in a game to throw behind the runner—for example, a base runner going first to third on a double or a batter who hits a sure double that he may try to stretch into a triple. If you sense a

Aggressive base runners provide the defense with opportunities to steal outs. Think of the tremendous lift this would give the pitcher after surrendering a single.

runner is going to round a base aggressively and there is no other play, look to throw to the base and catch him off-guard.

11. The first baseman should trail the runner on a sure double.

The batter launches a deep fly ball over the left fielder's head. The left fielder catches the ball, then hits the cutoff man, who turns and fires a strike to the first baseman at second.

First baseman at second? He's trailing the runner.

A sure double means the hitter definitely has second base and may try for a triple. If you're playing first base, there is no reason to occupy that position. The throw to the cutoff will be aligned to third base, so there is no chance of an overthrow that would be in the direction of the first-base position.

Once the middle infielders realize it's a sure double, they set up for a double cut. On a ball hit to left field, for example, the second baseman will vacate the base and position himself about 20 feet behind the shortstop cutoff (in case the ball gets past him or is thrown over his head). When playing first base, trail behind the runner and position yourself at second base. If the runner makes a big turn, the cutoff man can fire a throw behind him to second base.

This play is more likely to work on balls hit to left and left-center field. Because the ball is in front of the runner, he's emboldened to take a more aggressive turn. On balls behind him (right and right-center field), the third-base coach is holding him so he'll stop, turn, and look.

Trail the runner on sure doubles to take advantage of an overexcited offensive player.

12. Signal the catcher for a snap throw when the runner on first base is taking an aggressive secondary lead.

The pitch is thrown to the hitter, and moments after the catcher receives it, he snaps a throw down to first base. The runner on first barely gets back safely.

Did the play fail? Quite the contrary. It will have a positive effect throughout the rest of the game.

Runners are taught to take aggressive secondary leads off first base. It gives them a chance to advance on a ball in the dirt, beat the force play at second, go first to third on a base hit, or score on a double. If an aggressive secondary lead is so beneficial to the offense, then controlling (or limiting) their secondary leads would be equally beneficial to the defense.

Playing first base, you have the runner right in front of you. Pay attention to how far he's getting off base and also how he's landing. If his weight is carrying him toward second base as he lands, he's a prime candidate for a snap throw. (This can be difficult to see because you're watching the pitch, but when the hitter shows he's not swinging, immediately shift your eyes to the runner.)

Get the catcher's attention and give him a signal. It may be fixing your hat, tapping your glove, or something similar, and the catcher should have a return sign. As the pitch crosses home plate, sneak behind the runner to first base to set up the throw.

Even if the runner is safe, it has a lasting effect on that runner and his team. It sends a message that the catcher will throw to first if you get too much. That throw will make base runners think twice about getting an aggressive secondary lead. Try doing this early in the game if the opportunity is there.

Signaling the catcher should be something casual, such as wiping the sweat off your forehead.

Another great time for a snap throw to first is with multiple runners on base. You're often set up behind the runner, so he'll feel more secure. Secondary leads off first base are typically larger with runners on because the attention goes to the runners on second and third. Alert the catcher, sneak behind the runner on the pitch, and get your pitcher out of a jam.

13. When base coaches constantly shout to the runner on second, jab step toward second base as the pitcher begins his delivery.

With a runner on second base and two outs, the shortstop jab steps toward second base as the pitch is delivered. The coach yells, "Back!" and the runner shuffles toward second base. The batter lines a base hit to right field and the base coach holds the runner at third.

Why didn't he score? He had no secondary lead on the pitch.

If you're a middle infielder, keep your ears open for base coaches who constantly direct the runner at second base. You can use it to your team's advantage. Some coaches can be neurotic, yelling, "You're all right. Get another. Another step. Back one. You're OK. Back!"

When witnessing this, do as you normally would, keeping the runner close with your fellow middle infielder. Tap your glove, kick some dirt, take a step or two in and out. As soon as the pitcher begins his leg raise, take a hard jab step toward second base. Hold your positioning, but take a jab step and shift your body. This will lure the base coach to yell, "Back!" thinking an inside move is on.

Don't give up your positioning; just sell it with the jab step. Then bounce into your ready position. If the base runners are continually going back to the base on the pitch, they won't score on a base hit all day. It can make a big difference for your pitcher and the game's outcome.

Note: If the base coach tries to counter by not yelling "back," it's time to run a pickoff with the pitcher.

14. Adapt your positioning to the playing conditions.

The batter hits a ground ball to shortstop. The shortstop comes to the ball, fields it, and fires a strike to first base. The runner is safe.

Why is the runner safe? The grass was high and the shortstop was playing too deep.

Unless you're the pitcher or catcher, your positioning should change frequently throughout a game. The pitcher, batter, and game situation factor into whether you move right, left, up, or back. The field conditions, however, must also factor into the equation.

- *Sun.* Know where the sun is at all times throughout the game. The sun may not be a factor in the first inning, but it may become a factor in the sixth. Also, know who will have trouble with the sun at any given time during the game. If you're playing right field, for example, a fly ball to right-center field may not be in the sun. It may be in the eyes of the center fielder, though. He has a different angle. Don't give up on the ball; you may need to bail him out.
- *Wind.* When the wind blows out, the ball is going to carry farther. *Do not* coast with the ball or you'll get burned. Outfielders need to come hard on a pop-up to the infield because it may carry into the outfield. On pop-ups to the catcher, pitchers and corner infielders should also hustle in. If it carries out toward the field, call the catcher off.

  If the wind is blowing in, infielders should not assume the outfielder will get to a ball in the shallow outfield. The wind may hold it up and bring it back.

  If the ball is hit into the crosswinds, the crosswinds will carry the ball or hold it up. Crosswinds will have greater effect on balls that are hooked or sliced. If a left-handed hitter slices a ball to left field and the wind is blowing from right to left, the ball will slice and dive a greater amount.
- *Grass.* High grass calls for infielders to play a few steps up in the infield, especially with a quick runner at the plate. This also goes for double-play situations and plays at the plate. On the corners, look out for the bunt. Outfielders need to charge the ball hard on base hits because a heads-up base runner may try to stretch a ground-ball single into a double.

  With short grass, the infield plays fast. Infielders can play deeper to increase range. Be careful if the grass is wet. The ball may skip, so stay down and stay in front. You may also need to use a three-finger grip with a wet ball to ensure your accuracy.

- *Dirt.* The infield will play fast if the dirt is very dry or hard, so play deeper in the infield to give yourself more range and time to react. The ball will slow down and stay down in soft or wet dirt. In that instance, play a couple of steps in and stay down and through the ball. Don't assume you'll get a bounce.
- *Outfield fence.* With a short outfield fence, play a shallow outfield. Any ball that is hit deep will either be off or over the fence, so cut off the balls that drop short. Infielders also need to factor in the depth of the outfield when going out for a relay throw. Don't go out as deep and make the first throw a short one.

    With a deep or no outfield fence, play deeper in the outfield. A ball that gets by you may be rolling for a long time. Infielders may also have to go out farther, and the secondary middle infielder should look to release second base for the double cut.

    Lastly, outfielders should look for any potential strange kicks off the outfield fence. Angles in the corner or the type of fence (chain-link, wood, cement) will affect the bounce off the wall.

15. The catcher needs to give the "live" sign twice with a runner on second.

Every ball out of the pitcher's hand is getting pounded. Batters are right on every pitch.

Is his stuff that bad? Anything is possible, but the hitters may know what pitch is coming.

Baseball Etiquette: When an Umpire Is Hit by a Foul Tip, Talk to Your Pitcher

Foul tips that hit the umpire can be painful. No one should realize that more than a catcher. When this happens and you're the catcher, call time-out and visit the pitcher's mound. The purpose is to give the umpire time to recover.

An umpire will appreciate your actions and thank you for it. It's an act of humanity and will earn you the respect of the man behind the mask.

Base runners are taught to look in at the catcher's signs to the pitchers. If they pick up the sign, they will alert the hitter to what pitch is coming. As the catcher, you can't put down a single sign. That is obvious. When putting down a series of signs, however, you must put down the sign of the pitch you want thrown more than once. Putting it down once tips the runner.

For example, let's say you want the pitcher to throw a fastball. Your series of signs is two-one-two-three-wiggle. The pitcher throws a fastball. The second sign is the pitch being called. It's a simple process of elimination for the runner. With a series of one-two-one-one-three-two-wiggle, the live sign is flashed more than once. The runner won't know if it's the first, third, or fourth sign.

Pay attention to the signs you're putting down and assume the runner on second is doing the same. He may not be, but you need to make sure your pitcher is protected.

16. Guard the lines and allow nothing over your head late in the game with a one-run lead.

A hitter rips a ball down the third-base line. The third baseman moves a step to his right, fields the ball, and fires to first for the out.

What was he doing there? He was there to defend a potential extra-base hit.

If you're a corner infielder, take a couple of steps toward the foul line and back in the final inning of a one-run game. (How deep you can play at third base depends on your arm strength.) Don't stand on the line, but you should be comfortable that you'll be able to stop any ball hit down the line. The reason is your team wants to prevent a double, which puts the tying run in scoring position.

It's true that this leaves a bigger hole between short and third and first and second. However, a single keeps the runner at first. It takes two hits or an extra-base hit to score the runner. If the batter doubles down the line, a single hit can score the runner and tie the game.

As an outfielder, play deeper in this situation. Position yourself so you can keep everything in front of you and cut balls off that are hit toward the gap. If the ball gets past you or over your head, it's a sure double and the runner is in scoring position.

17. Don't take your bat out onto the field with you.

The third baseman strikes out for the second time with runners in scoring position. He takes the field, and on the very first play of the inning a ground ball is hit to him. He fields it, cocks his arm, and fires a throw that sails high and right into the bleachers.

Why did he try to throw the ball so hard? He was still angry about his previous at-bat.

Don't let this happen. It's a sign of an immature player. Although it's understandable to be disappointed or frustrated after a bad at-bat, you've got to let it go when you take the field. Don't compound the problem by allowing your emotions to adversely affect your concentration and execution on defense.

The great thing about baseball is that there are so many ways to contribute to a win: a hit, taking an extra base on a weak outfield arm, a bunt, turning a double play, or hitting the cutoff man. Great players find more than one way to win baseball games.

In spite of this, position players commonly gauge their performance by their offensive stat line. "How did you play today?" Out of 100 responses, 99 will be something like, "I did OK. I was 1-for-3 with a double." The question was how did you *play*, not how did you *hit*. Defense is as important, if not more so, as your offensive performance. Saving a run counts just the same on the scoreboard as driving one in. As stated by Gold Glove–winning first baseman Keith Hernandez, "I win a game with my glove just as easily as I can with my bat."

Keep in mind that for the majority of the game, you have a glove on your hand. You'd better be good at it or the coach will get someone else to play, especially at higher levels of the game. If your offense is sputtering, make a great defensive play in the field. You'll maintain your value to the team as well as your spot in the lineup.

18. Look for a pickoff play when your pitcher is in a jam.

The bases are loaded with one out in a tight game. The leadoff hitter (right-handed) is at the plate. The pitcher throws a pitch up and away and the catcher fires a snap throw to nail the runner at first base.

Isn't this risky with the bases loaded? The defense getting offensive in a tight spot is a more accurate description.

When an offense gets on a roll, it has a tendency to snowball. Hitters feel more confident at the plate, base runners are more aggressive, and fielders tend to get back on their heels. When you sense this is happening, look to put on a pickoff play. It can help the pitcher out of a tight spot and quickly shift the momentum of the game. "The thing about a pickoff play is not just the 26 or 27 guys you get a year—and I don't want to minimize that—but it just kills a ballclub," said former Baltimore Orioles manager and pitching coach Ray Miller. "It happens to us every once in a while, and you can just hear the club go flat."

The best target for a pickoff play is the trail runner, as the attention on the baseball field always goes to the lead runner. He is the base runner of greatest concern because he's the closest to scoring. Trail runners sense this and mentally relax. They feel as if they're safe in the distant background.

Diversionary tactics create the best chance to pick runners. This entails participation from teammates away from the pickoff play and timing on behalf of the pitcher and player at the base. Cause commotion near the lead runner so it draws even greater attention, and then quickly administer a precision strike on the trail runner.

Here are a few examples of base runners to target and pick when your pitcher is struggling.

- Runners on first and second. Have a middle infielder create commotion by breaking toward second base for a possible pickoff while the first baseman sneaks behind the runner at first. The pitcher jump pivots and fires to first.
- Runners on first and second base in a bunt situation. Without drawing attention, the second baseman positions himself deeper and shades toward first base. The first baseman charges in early for the bunt, giving the runner on first a greater sense of security. The second baseman breaks to first when the pitcher begins his delivery. The catcher receives a pitchout and snaps a throw to first base for the pickoff.
- Runners on second and third base. The third baseman is playing off the base. The pitcher sets and holds for a couple of seconds, allowing the base runners to get to a maximum lead. The third baseman breaks for third and calls out. The second

The eyes of the runner on first base (and the first-base coach) are drawn to the commotion at second base. This is when the first baseman cuts behind the runner for the pickoff. Pickoff plays work best when the entire infield is alert and involved.

baseman quietly breaks for second base behind the runner. The pitcher spins and throws to second.

- Bases are loaded. This is a great time to target the runner on first or second base. In this situation their primary and secondary leads are typically bigger. Run a pick play with the pitcher or call for a snap throw from the catcher.

Again, when the wheels are coming off and the opponent is building toward a big inning, get offensive on defense. Prey on their excitement and anticipation. Play dead and then strike down the trail runner. It will lift up your pitcher and defense and deflate the offensive team.

19. With two outs and a runner on first, the shortstop should play deeper than usual.

With two outs and a runner on first base, the batter bounces a ball up the middle. The shortstop ranges to his left, gloves the ball, and flips it to second for the force-out.

How did he get to the ball? He took advantage of there being a force at second base.

Positioning in the field is critical to optimizing your range. Your positioning is determined by your agility, speed, and arm strength. Field conditions and the batter are also items to consider along with the game situation. With two outs and a runner on first base, the easiest play for a shortstop is to get the force at second base.

Because the throw to second is shorter than the throw to first, play deeper at shortstop. It increases your range and strengthens your team defense. Whether the ball is hit deep in the shortstop hole or up the middle, it can take a potential base hit away and close out the inning.

Keep in mind that by playing deep, the ball is going to take more time to get to you. It is essential that you field and release the ball in a timely fashion, particularly when a fast runner is on first base. With that, come to the ball whenever possible. If you gain ground on the ball, you'll receive it earlier and deliver it quicker to second base.

20. Look in to see the catcher's signs and location so you know the pitch being thrown.

The count is 1-1 on a left-handed hitter. The pitcher throws a breaking ball and it's pulled into the first-base hole. The second baseman takes a couple of steps to his left, fields the ball, and throws to first for the out.

What was the second baseman doing so far over? He looked in at the catcher's signs.

Positioning is as important as speed and arm strength on defense. Infielders and outfielders should look in at the signs to adjust their positioning according to the pitch being thrown.

The logic is simple. Breaking balls and changeups are slower pitches and generally pulled. Fastballs are not pulled as often but are more typically hit to the location they're thrown. Adjust your positioning accordingly. This will not be the case 100 percent of the time, but more often than not, you'll be in better position than if you stand in the same spot all game.

Other factors must be taken into consideration as well: the velocity of the pitcher's pitches, the types of breaking balls he throws, the bat speed of the hitter, his mechanics, and field conditions. These elements combined with the catcher's sign to the pitcher weigh into where you position yourself with each delivery.

Changeups are much more likely to be pulled by the hitter. Quietly adjust your position in the field.

Don't adjust your positioning too early. If a hitter notices you moving before the pitch, it can tip him off to what is coming. Either shift in a casual manner or wait until the pitcher begins his delivery to move.

Outfielders need to look in as well because they have more ground to cover. It's not necessary to know the precise pitch; just look for one finger or multiple fingers (fastball or off-speed). If you're a wing outfielder and can't see the signs, ask an infielder to relay the sign. Adjusting his brim, for example, means an off-speed pitch is being thrown and no adjustment is a fastball.

Stay in the game and think along with the pitcher and catcher. You'll increase your range and be able to anticipate better.

21. On a ground ball hit deep in the shortstop hole with runners on first and second, look to throw behind the runner at third.

With runners on first and second base, a ground ball is hit deep in the shortstop hole. The shortstop backhands the ball, stops, and flips the ball to third base.

Why would he throw to third with no chance of getting the force-out? Because he's throwing behind the runner.

On this play, the runner on second has to go on contact and knows he has third base. What he does not know is if the ball is going to get through to the outfield. The ball is behind him. If it does get through, he has to score. Because of this, he may take a turn around third base.

As the shortstop, chances are you'll have no play at first or even second base. So quickly turn your attention to third base. If the third baseman did not go after the ball, his instincts should take him to the third-base bag. If the runner doesn't slide and has momentum heading into third base, flip a throw behind him. Getting the lead runner here would be a huge play.

A long throw to first base from shortstop on this play can really backfire, especially if you have little to no chance of getting the runner. The base runner from second base, if he's a heads-up player, can continue running and score on the play if you make that long throw to first.

22. On a deep fly ball that drifts foul with a runner on third with less than two outs, let the ball drop.

With the score tied 5–5 in the eighth inning, the batter sends a deep fly ball to right field near foul territory. There is one out and a runner on third base. The right fielder gets under the ball and lets it drop.

Is this the right play? In this situation, it's definitely the right play.

In most cases, any time you have an opportunity to secure an out, take it. This is an exception to the rule. Before letting the ball drop, however, you have to be absolutely sure of two things: (1) the ball will definitely land foul and (2) it's deep enough where you'll have no shot at throwing out the runner at home plate.

To be sure of this, you have to know the base runner and your arm strength. After factoring those two elements in, if you're convinced you have no chance to throw the runner out, let the ball go. There's no damage done, and if your team gets out of the inning without that runner scoring, they'll all be thanking you for it.

23. Take note of the base runner's mannerisms as he takes his leads—he might tip that he's stealing.

The runner on first gets out to his lead. As the pitcher lifts his leg, he takes off for second. The catcher steps out, receives the pitchout, and guns the runner down at second.

The first lead (top) indicates the runner is holding at first base. The second lead begs for the pitcher to hold and step off, throw over to first, or pitch out.

Does he have the signs from the third-base coach? It's possible, or he may have taken advantage of a giveaway from the runner.

When playing catcher, you're the lone position player facing the field. The runner at first base presents a challenge to you because he may run. Watch him as he takes his leads to see if you can anticipate a steal. Here are a few things to look for.

- He gets out to his lead much earlier so that he's guaranteed to get his optimum lead.
- He takes longer getting the sign and then rushes out to a big lead.
- His lead is significantly larger than his previous leads.
- He appears "runnerish," meaning he looks more intense with his body language and shows greater concentration on the pitcher. He's coiled and ready to spring into action.
- His set position is lower and his feet are wider apart.

These observations commonly occur after the pitcher has his sign. If a player tips that he's running, there are a couple of "audibles" you can call. Have the pitcher step off or throw over. Observe the runner's body language because he may flinch toward second and confirm your suspicion. On the ensuing pitch, you have the option to call for a pitchout or a fastball to your throwing side. This gives you your best shot to throw out the runner.

When a pitcher steps off or throws over, the coach may remove the steal sign or the runner may decide himself not to go. If this is the case, mission accomplished. You've stopped him from even attempting to steal second. Stopping a team from stealing before they even make the attempt is the best way to shut down a running game. It's 100 percent effective.

24. Watch your depth when you're the opposite-field outfielder.

A left-handed leadoff hitter stands at the plate. He slices the ball into short left field for a sure single. The left fielder takes a few steps in and catches the ball for the out.

What was he doing playing so shallow? He did a great job positioning himself.

Balls hit to the opposite field are not hit as hard or as far as balls to center or the pull side. Because the ball is hit deeper in the hitting zone, the hitter has less time (and space) to generate bat speed. Position yourself shallower when you're covering the opposite field.

The other factor is that most balls tail or fade when hit to the opposite field. The ball often dies toward the foul line. If you begin with less depth, you'll take away those cheap hits that drive pitchers crazy.

Ranking Tools by Position

As your career progresses, your physical strengths should match your primary position. By also taking your weaknesses into account, you should be able to isolate a position or two that are best suited to your individual abilities. (Left-handed fielders, unfortunately, are limited to first base, outfield, and pitcher.)

The following chart identifies how professional organizations and college programs rank the importance of each of the five baseball tools by position.

Key: 1—field; 2—throw; 3—bat; 4—power; 5—speed

POSITION	ORDER OF RANK
Catcher	1, 2, 3, 4, 5
First base	3, 4, 1, 2, 5
Second base	3, 1, 5, 4, 2
Shortstop	1, 2, 5, 3, 4
Third base	3, 4, 1, 2, 5
Left field	4, 3, 5, 1, 2
Center field	5, 1, 3, 2, 4
Right field	3, 4, 1, 2, 5

4
Pitching

Pitchers are always in search of ways to improve themselves in the off-season. They work on fine-tuning their mechanics to maximize velocity and gain consistent command of their pitches. They train in the weight room so their body is better prepared to remain healthy, to throw harder, and to build endurance and confidence. They will commonly work on a new pitch that will enhance their repertoire to foil hitters.

If you're a pitcher, these are all sensible objectives that will augment your pitching prowess. How many of them, however, will be of service when you don't have your stuff? Which of them will bail you out of a bases-loaded jam when the hitter already has two hits off you? What new pitch will give you a plan to attack the weakness of a hitter you've never faced before? There is more to pitching than a sound delivery and lighting up the radar gun.

To continue to improve and to continue pitching, you have to open your mind and become really good at things besides your pitches. Holding runners, situational pitching, maintaining composure, reading hitters, and fielding your position are just a few skills that make you better at playing the game. There is no position out on the field that is more important than the pitcher's position. Your job is not just to throw pitches, but also to think and play the game.

Two perfect examples of pitchers who play the game are Greg Maddux and Pedro Martinez. They have seven Cy Young Awards between them. Martinez has exceptional stuff, but did you know that he is better at holding runners on than any right-handed pitcher in the game? Martinez will hold the ball long, step off, and vary his deliveries to home plate. When a runner gets on base, Martinez has a side game with the runner that he plans to win each time, and usually he does.

Maddux has good stuff and great command, but he exposes hitters by reading their takes and mannerisms. "The Professor" executes his pitches based on what he's observed. Maddux also has 17 Gold Gloves in his trophy case. If you think these strengths that Martinez and Maddux possess don't contribute to wins, think again. They are competitors and pursue all means to get an edge.

Adding sixth-tool qualities to your makeup will help you avoid trouble and, when you're in trouble, help you out of it. If you've pitched, you're well aware of those days when your fastball is flat, your breaking ball has no bite, and your command is suspect. What do you do in this situation? Hold up a white flag and tell the hitters to take it easy on you? No, you go to the well and figure out ways to get outs. Pick a runner off, exploit a hitter who appears anxious, shake the catcher off in sure-fastball counts, and slow the pace of the game down. Always remember there are two categories of players that represent potential outs on the baseball field: hitters and base runners. When you're having trouble getting the hitters, seek out some base runners.

The pitcher is the lone player on your team who will have a *W* or *L* next to his name once the outcome is decided. Be really good at everything to give yourself the best chance of cozying up to that *W* on a regular basis. There will be games in which your pitches will carry your performance and your sixth-tool skills can stay on the shelf. But where you're challenged by a tough opponent or your pitches just aren't there, you need to call on all means necessary to come out ahead.

Tips for Taking the Mound

The following tips will help pitchers achieve success using weapons other than a crackling fastball or a sharp breaking pitch. They don't tax the arm but rather challenge the pitcher to tap into his senses.

1. Shake the catcher off in textbook fastball counts.

With the bases loaded and the 5-hitter at the plate, the pitcher runs the count to 2-0. He does not want to go to 3-0 and be one pitch away from walking a run in, so he's going to throw his most accurate pitch: a fastball. The pitcher toes the rubber, stares in at the sign, and shakes it off. He shakes again before nodding "yes" to the catcher. He delivers the pitch and the hitter is just late, lofting a short fly ball to the opposite field.

Was it a flawed swing or great pitch? Neither. It was doubt on behalf of the hitter.

In this sequence, the catcher is giving the pitcher "the horns," which alerts him to shake off the catcher. (The horns is when the pinkie and pointer finger are extended down.) It's simply for show, but the purpose is to create doubt in the mind of the hitter. Because the batter is convinced he can sit on a fastball in this situation, why not mess with him a little bit? He now begins to question why the pitcher is shaking off signs. "Is he going to throw something off-speed because he knows I'm sitting fastball?"

Confusion and uncertainty reign when we don't follow—or don't seem to follow—predictable patterns. That subtle doubt is what can make the hitter a hair late on the incoming fastball. A slight hesitation reading the pitch and then tensing up when rushing to catch up to the fastball makes the barrel late. That is enough to jam the hitter or make him just tardy enough to avoid catching the ball square.

With the count 2-0, you merely threw the 2-0 fastball that everyone was predicting. But because you went through the simple exercise of shaking off the catcher before delivering the pitch, your fastball gained three or four miles per hour. The batter is out and now you can focus on getting ahead of the next hitter.

2. Read the hitter before the swing.

The batter sets in his stance with a lot of movement. His hands are circling rapidly and his front foot is tapping. He appears very anxious.

How does the pitcher attack the hitter? Off-speed pitches and pitches away.

Every hitter has strengths and weaknesses at the plate. It's your job as the pitcher to determine his strengths and then exploit his weaknesses. The hitter's batting stance is a good place to start. Look for extremes, such as holding his hands high or low, a wide or narrow base, an open or closed stance. These are general indicators as to what type of pitches and pitch locations might give him trouble.

With the exception of professional baseball, scouting reports on hitters are not often available. As a pitcher, the only information you'll get is what the hitter shows you before you make a pitch. Below is a list of tips to look for in hitters' stance descriptions that may provide you with a plan of attack.

- High hand position—difficult time hitting pitches down in the strike zone; particularly down and inside
- Low hand position—difficult time squaring off on pitches up in the strike zone
- Closed shoulders or feet—tough time with inside strikes
- Open stance—trouble with outside part of the strike zone
- Rapid or excessive movement in stance—a sign of anxiousness, commonly struggles with off-speed pitches
- Wide stance—trouble with pitches up in the strike zone
- Narrow stance—commonly drifts, meaning trouble with off-speed and pitches down in the strike zone.
- Flat (horizontal) bat position—tough time with pitches down in the zone and inside strikes
- Vertical bat position—difficulty with pitches up in the strike zone

With a flat bat and closed stance, this hitter
will have trouble with inside fastballs.

3. Read the hitter during the swing.

*The batter begins in a square stance, but his front foot lands open with
the stride.*

*How should the pitcher attack this hitter? Fastballs away and
pitches that break away from him.*

A batter can set up in a textbook batting stance, but his fundamentals may break down during the preswing or swing. Pay attention to what the hitter shows you with his swings and his takes.

While there may be no noticeable flaws in the hitter's mechanics, he still reveals his swing path and bat speed when he pulls the
trigger. This can also tell you what pitches he can or cannot handle.
Some hitters may do everything right but simply don't possess the
fast-twitch muscle fibers that allow them to swing that quickly. With
that, a long swing path makes a hitter vulnerable to fastballs and
off-speed pitches.

Here are some things to look for when the hitter takes a pitch or
takes a swing:

If the hitter pulls your fastball foul, try pitching below his bat speed with something off-speed.

- Strides open—vulnerable to outside strikes and pitches that move away from him
- Strides close—can have a tough time with hard pitches in and pitches down
- High leg kick—difficulty adjusting to change of speeds
- Long stride—difficult time with breaking pitches, inside fastballs, and high fastballs
- Wrapping the bat in the load—trouble hitting inside fastballs and/or keeping them fair
- Hitch (drops hands)—tough time hitting pitches up in the strike zone
- Premature weight shift (gets out front)—trouble with off-speed pitches and inside fastballs
- Casting out (long swing)—difficulty with inside strikes
- Uppercut swing—vulnerable to low and high strikes
- Descending (downward) swing—trouble handling low and inside strikes

4. Read the hitter after the swing.

A batter takes an aggressive swing at a fastball and fouls it straight back. He appears upset with himself, pounds the plate with his bat, and quickly digs his feet back in the box.

Should you challenge with another fastball? Not if you're paying attention to what he's telling you.

The previous two tips discussed countering a hitter's physical shortcomings. This is about exposing a hitter's emotions. Paying attention to facial expressions, body language, and hesitations in thought can give you a sense of direction. Angry, excited, or anxious hitters typically struggle with off-speed pitches and pitches on the outer half of the plate. You may even consider locating pitches that border the strike zone to see if the hitter will chase. Timid, nervous hitters or those who appear to be deep in thought between pitches can be attacked with velocity.

Below are a few general descriptions of mood and how the hitter can be pursued.

- Anxious—pitches out of the strike zone or off-speed
- Angry—off-speed pitches, high fastballs, pitches out of the strike zone
- Timid—fastballs inside and up in the strike zone
- Tense—fastballs inside and off-speed pitches away

5. Continue to challenge the hitter with fastballs if he hasn't proven he can catch up.

A hitter swings late on a fastball for strike one. He's late on the next fastball and fouls it off. With the count 0-2, the pitcher throws a change-up and the batter strokes a base hit to center field.

Was it a bad pitch? It was poor pitch selection by the pitcher.

Read this out loud. "If a hitter can't seem to catch up to my fastball, I am not going to speed his bat up by throwing an off-speed pitch. I will attack him with fastballs in." If the batter can't catch up, don't help him.

Nothing drives a coach crazier than when a pitcher dominates a hitter with his fastball early in the count and then gets cute with an off-speed pitch. Don't feel as if you have to fool a hitter to get him out. If he can't handle the juice, punish him with hard stuff.

6. "Hold" the ball against legitimate base stealers.

A base stealer is on first base and has the steal sign. The pitcher stretches and comes set. He holds for one second, two seconds, three seconds, four seconds. . . . Finally, he delivers the pitch to home plate.

The runner gets a terrible jump and is thrown out by the catcher. Why? Because the pitcher did a good job of "holding the runner."

If you ask a world-class sprinter, he'll tell you that he prefers it when a starter fires the gun shortly after yelling "set." When the starter holds the runners in the set position for a long time, runners often false-start. There is too much tension and anxiety building. This idea holds true for base stealers.

When you're on the mound, keep in mind that there is no time clock in baseball. You dictate the pace of the game and determine when to deliver to home plate. Holding the runner on first base is not just about throwing over to first. It's also about disrupting the runner's timing.

Base runners hate it when the pitcher holds the ball long. Tension inevitably creeps into their body and the first step loses quickness and explosiveness. Runners also like to get into a rhythm, and when the pitcher is constantly changing his holds, the base runner can't time or anticipate when to take off.

Holding the ball in the set position irritates base stealers. It doesn't allow them to time your delivery and creates tension in their lead position.

Taking it a step further, come set, hold the ball long, and eventually step back off the rubber. This not only frustrates the runner but also may tip you to whether he's definitely stealing on the pitch. He may flinch or false start. When this is witnessed, the coach has the option of calling a pitchout.

As a bonus, the batter doesn't like you holding the ball either. He becomes tense and his eyes grow tired waiting to lock into the pitch.

7. When in doubt, pitch the ball to the location where it is most difficult for the batter to hit the ball powerfully: down and away.

A phenomenal hitter is at the plate and he's red hot. Runners are on first and second base with two outs. The pitcher throws a fastball on the low and outside corner and the batter hits a hard ground ball to second base for the final out.

What was the secret? The pitcher threw the ball in a great location.

Bonds, Pujols, Guerrero, Rodriguez. Not a fun list of guys to face. Leagues at all levels have their versions of these dangerous hitters, and they have to be pitched to. So how do you approach pitching the most dangerous of hitters?

A trap pitchers fall into is thinking they should flood dangerous hitters with buckets of off-speed pitches. The problem with that is the very best hitters have been served a steady diet of breaking pitches throughout their careers. Because they've seen so many, they are better at recognizing them and better at hitting them. Manny Ramirez has launched bushels of breaking pitches over the Green Monster. Manny may not always articulate how he hits them so well, but it's a combination of his ability to sense a breaking pitch is coming, recognizing it, and tattooing it.

When a great hitter has no known weakness, attack the low and outside part of the strike zone. It's not a location that a hitter can do a whole lot with. He may drive a base hit the other way, but if the ball is kept at the knees on the outer half, it's pretty much all he'll do with it. And even to drive that pitch to the opposite field, the hitter has to do a lot of things right.

Furthermore, hitters will typically take that pitch. So if you can locate your fastball in that spot and get called strikes, you'll find

Every Great Pitcher Is a Closer

A closer is a pitcher who comes in late in a close game to earn a save. His team has a marginal lead of three runs or less, and he enters from the bullpen to close the book on another victory.

Every good pitcher is a closer, but not under that precise definition. Successful pitchers are able to close out hitters and close innings. There are 27 batters to close out in a game and nine innings to close. Great pitchers can sense the door closing on a hitter or inning, and they're able to slam that door shut. It's a mentality they possess on the mound.

When a pitcher gets two strikes on a batter, he needs to smell blood and go after him. It's not a time to play around or relax. The hitter is staggering and it's time to deliver the knockout punch. Don't give him life by letting him off the ropes. Go with your out pitch or attack him with a fastball.

Nothing is more frustrating than a pitcher getting the first two outs of an inning and then walking the following hitter. It's a total loss of concentration and lack of killer instinct. Think about what's going on in the offense's dugout after the first two hitters make outs. They're picking up gloves and preparing to head out to the field—they've given up! Don't give them any reason for hope. Get after the hitter and close the inning out.

Some hitters and innings are tougher to close out than others. This presents a test of character for the pitcher. Can he tap into all his available resources to close it out, or will he falter when challenged?

You may be tabbed a starter, but consider yourself a closer at all times. Anyone can start an inning. Only the best walk back to the dugout after the third out is recorded.

yourself ahead in the count more often than behind. (If you can't hit the outside corner at the knees, practice it in the bullpen.) When facing a dangerous hitter, the one place you don't want to find yourself is behind in the count.

Pitching around hitters, or the unintentional intentional walk, is a growing trend in baseball. Many times it's unnecessary. Granted there are game situations when you should work around hitters, but don't treat them like they're invincible. If you make a good pitch, the odds are in your favor. Round ball with a round bat and eight defenders of the field? I like your chances.

8. Learn to pitch below bat speed.

A right-handed hitter rips a fastball foul down the left-field line. The pitcher comes back with a changeup and gets a weak ground ball to shortstop.

What did the pitcher learn? He learned that pitching above the hitter's bat speed was not an option.

There are three speeds you can throw to a hitter. You can throw above bat speed, at bat speed, or below bat speed. In some cases, you may have the ability to throw above bat speed. This depends on the velocity of your fastball and the hitter's bat speed. At times, however, you may be unable to throw above bat speed (that is, blow the ball by the hitter). In these cases you have to learn to throw below bat speed.

More major league pitchers do this than you think. Thoughts immediately go to guys such as Jamie Moyer, Tom Glavine, or Livan Hernandez. But Johan Santana, Roger Clemens, and Curt Schilling also pitch below bat speed when necessary. Santana throws his *changeup* so far below bat speed that hitters can sometimes guess changeup and still swing early.

The name of the game in pitching is outs. Strikeouts are sexy, but outs of any kind are of the utmost importance. Gearing up and throwing a fastball by a hitter is also sexy, but getting him to slow his swing down and hit a weak pop-up is just as effective.

Keep in mind also that throwing the ball below bat speed will produce a lot of one-pitch outs. Throwing the ball above bat speed entails a minimum of three pitches. In this day and age where pitch counts are heavily scrutinized, strikeout or power pitchers find themselves out of the game by the sixth inning. Pitchers who induce hits on weak swings keep their pitch counts down and compete deeper into games.

Not everyone can decide to crank it up to throw above bat speed. When facing special hitters, it's impossible. Learn to pitch below bat speed and no hitter will be impossible to conquer.

9. Fooling the hitter can set him up for the next pitch.

On a 1-1 count, the pitcher throws the hitter a breaking ball. The hitter is anticipating or reads fastball and is fooled badly on the pitch. He gets way out on his front foot and weakly swings and misses. The batter steps out and practices his stride, demonstrating a mind-set of staying back and getting better against off-speed pitches. The pitcher comes back with an inside fastball and freezes the hitter for a called third strike.

Why not throw another breaking pitch? Because the hitter showed he was concerned about the breaking pitch.

Hitters do not like to look bad. As mentioned in the opening chapter, human nature factors into how players approach the game, and when a hitter gets fooled, his initial instinct is that he doesn't want to get fooled again.

As the pitcher, you need to take this into consideration. Observe what the hitter is showing you. Conventional thought is the hitter just missed your breaking pitch badly, so throw another until he proves he can handle it. This may work early in your career, but more experienced players will adjust. They've seen more breaking pitches and are less likely to bite twice.

An off-speed pitch away helps set up a fastball inside.

A hitter who steps out of the batter's box and practices taking a short strike (staying back) is primed for an inside fastball. He is trying to tell you how to get him out by his actions. They say, "I'm going to see the ball long and keep my weight back as long as possible." There is no better time to pump a hard pitch inside. Often the hitter will freeze and take the third strike. Even if he does get the bat off his shoulder and swing, he'll fail to get the barrel out front and he'll get jammed.

There is one caveat. It is important to know your enemy. There are times you give hitters too much credit in terms of assuming they'll make an adjustment. Simply put, there are hitters who are plain dumb and don't even attempt to think along with what's happening. In this case, a breaking ball that fools the hitter may just as easily fool him again. It's the "thinker" who will try to make adjustments from pitch to pitch.

10. In a bases-loaded jam, you're one pitch away.
The bases are loaded with one out and the cleanup hitter is at the plate. The opposing team is up off the bench and the fans are cheering in anticipation of a big hit.

Is the pitcher in serious trouble? No. He's one pitch away from getting out of the inning unscathed.

Pitching is not just about stuff. It's also a state of mind. In this precise situation, pitchers tend to get nervous, scared, or apprehensive. They become so overwhelmed with what might happen that they lose focus on what they need to do to keep those things from happening.

As the pitcher in this scenario, you're one good pitch away. Understand the hitter is looking to drive the ball to the outfield, so first things first, keep the ball down. He may try to help the ball get up in the air, top it, and now you've got the ground-ball double play you're looking for. Off-speed pitches that are located at the knees also produce a lot of ground balls. A ground ball, pop-up, line-out, strikeout—any of these outcomes will work. Make one good pitch and you're likely to get a favorable outcome.

Hitters are anxious with the bases soaked, so play off their emotions rather than allowing yours to muddle your thoughts. And remember, if the coach didn't think you could make one good pitch, he'd replace you.

11. When in trouble, look for pick plays.

With runners on second and third and nobody out, the pitcher looks in for the sign from the catcher. He comes set, looks back at the runner at second, glances at the runner at third, counts to one, and executes an inside move to pick the runner off second base.

Was this a heads-up pitcher or foolish base runner? It's a smart pitcher getting himself out of a jam without throwing a pitch.

When times are tight in a ballgame, utilize all of your resources to fight back. Base runners are sniffing out home plate and are primed for trickery. Pick plays can get you out of a jam and shift momentum back in your favor.

You've been there before. A ground-ball single followed by a double in the gap has the opposing offense energized. The team is more vocal and the base runners are more opportunistic. A quick rally has a tendency to diminish fear, and suddenly base runners become more vulnerable. They have landed a few jabs and are looking to deliver the knockout punch. Great time to counterpunch.

This is a time for the wily side of you to step forward. Play into the excitement. Display some signs of bad body language to appear as if you're rattled and defeated. This will give the base runners an even greater sense of comfort and arrogance.

Often the best base runner to target is the trail runner. The attention always seems to go to the runner closest to home plate (both by the offense and the defense), so the trail runner is the individual poised for a sneak attack.

You are the key to this play, so you can't be consumed with your troubles. Keep your head up and look for a quick momentum changer. A subtle signal, such as a wipe of the brow or grabbing the rosin bag, can let teammates know a pickoff play is in the works. Now they can begin their role of making the runners feel safe. Outfielders should also be aware of potential pick plays. This gives the pitcher greater comfort in zipping a low throw to a base, knowing the outfielder will be in position to back up.

Another option is for the catcher to snap throw to a base following a pitch. With runners on first and second, for example, the runner on first often bounces to a large secondary lead. The first baseman is typically playing behind him, which enables the runner to take a big primary lead to start. With you, the catcher, and the first baseman all in cahoots, throw a fastball off the plate (to the first-base side), giving the catcher an opportunity to throw behind the runner. You may get yourself a quick out that breaks the back of the offense.

Nothing deflates a rally faster than a pick play.

12. Practice situational pitching.

A pitcher is in a tight jam and needs to get a ground ball out of the hitter. He throws three consecutive pitches at the knees toward the outer half of the plate. The hitter finally rolls a ground ball to the shortstop.

How was he able to locate his pitches with such consistency? He has practiced pitching in this situation in the bullpen.

There are several reasons pitchers practice in the bullpen. They polish their delivery, maintain feel of their arsenal of pitches, and condition their arms. All of these items represent a purpose for side-work. A final component that should be addressed is pitching to specific game situations. Hitters do it, and pitchers should include it as a critical portion of their practice to improve game execution.

The list of game situations you can practice is endless. Your menu of items to select can be based on your recent history of performance (situations that arose in your last few outings) along with situations you may encounter. One bullpen session may focus on 0-2 out pitches, locating a pitch in hopes of producing a double-play ground ball, and 3-2 changeups. In addition, be sure to vary who you are facing: a left-handed hitter or a right-handed hitter, a power hitter or a contact hitter, a patient hitter or an anxious hitter. Need a strikeout? Understand how you can best get one, and practice it over and over. This is especially important if you're a pitcher who doesn't normally strike out many hitters.

It is also important to practice situational pitches out of the strike zone. A common location pitchers target is a fastball up and inside, hoping to get the hitter to chase. To hit that spot consistently, you need to practice throwing to that location against right-handed and left-handed hitters. A curveball that breaks down and off the plate is another example of practicing a pitch that lands out of the strike zone.

Practice situational pitching in the bullpen so you'll feel comfortable when you need it in the game. This also makes bullpens

It can be helpful to have a hitter stand in at the plate during a bullpen session. Also, throw the majority of your pitches from the stretch position.

more fun. Make it a running contest with all the guys on the staff. You'll get to find out which situations you handle best and which you need to improve on.

13. Be accurate outside the strike zone.

A pitcher throws four pitches to a batter. The fourth pitch is on a 1-2 count and the batter taps a ground ball to shortstop for an out.

All four pitches were out of the strike zone. Is the pitcher wild? Not exactly. He's accurate outside of the strike zone.

Coaches talk about pitchers being wild in the strike zone. What they mean by that is the pitches are getting too much of the middle of the plate. Despite the fact that the pitcher is throwing strikes, they are not quality strikes that are located in an area that troubles the hitter.

The flip side of that is being accurate outside of the strike zone. Anxious hitters have a tendency to chase pitches, so if they don't possess the discipline to lay off balls out of the strike zone, why throw them anything in the strike zone? In addition, these pitches can serve as purpose pitches that set up another pitch. Here are a few examples:

- Getting a hitter to climb the ladder up and then out of the strike zone
- Moving the hitter's feet to get him feeling uncomfortable
- Breaking ball in the dirt to see if he'll chase
- Changeup down and away to get a rollover ground ball
- Fastball up and in to get a pop-up with runners in scoring position
- Expanding the strike zone in an attempt to get calls from the umpire off the plate

It is important, however, that you're *accurate* outside the strike zone. Pitches far outside of the zone won't get even free swingers to bite. They must be inviting enough so that hitters will commit to starting their hands. If this sounds easy, it's not! Few pitchers spend time learning to throw balls. But they should.

Aggressive hitters are targets, but game situations can make even the most patient hitters overanxious as well. A runner on third base with less than two outs is a perfect example. A batter is hoping to get a pitch to drive. Use that to your advantage. Know he needs to get the barrel out to drive the ball and will commit to swing a fraction sooner. Throw a pitch that's just off the plate and you'll set him up to get himself out.

14. Throw first-pitch strikes.

The batter takes his stance at the plate and is set to begin his at-bat. The pitcher fires a first-pitch fastball down the middle for strike one.

Is this as simple as it seems? For the most part, yes it is.

As 1990 AL Cy Young Award winner Bob Welch once said, "The game is the count." Pitching from an 0-1 count has many advantages when compared with 1-0. When a pitcher throws strike one from the onset, he takes command of the at-bat. A pitcher who becomes offensive forces the hitter to become defensive.

Hitting coaches will tell batters until they're blue in the face about jumping on a first-pitch fastball. They explain how the pitcher wants to get ahead, how a fastball is his most accurate pitch, and how he counts on the hitter taking the first pitch. Yet most hitters continue to lock up and see the pitch for a strike. A straight take sign may be in effect, the hitter may be concerned with making a one-pitch out, or he might feel he needs to time a pitch and see the point of release before taking a hack. Whatever the case may be, the majority of hitters will take the first pitch, so take advantage.

Some hitters pride themselves on being aggressive early in the count. Keep in mind that middle of the strike zone is not the suggested target. Split the zone in quadrants and aim for a region: up and inside, down and inside, up and outside, down and outside. Force the hitter to determine whether the pitch is a good enough strike to attack. The batter will often become too anxious and chase a pitch outside his hitting zone (or desired area of the strike zone).

You should also keep in mind that if a hitter does swing on the first pitch and connects, there are seven fielders behind you to make a play. If an out is recorded, you achieved it with one pitch. A majority of balls hit fair are outs, and the best out is a quick out. Fielders love guys who pitch ahead, and they play better defense.

The difference between 1-0 and 0-1 is the difference between the sun and the dark side of the moon.

15. Don't snap the ball, don't stare at the umpire, and don't vocalize your thoughts.

With the count 2-2, the pitcher fires a fastball that freezes the hitter and borders the inside corner of the plate. The umpire remains motionless, much to the chagrin of the pitcher. The catcher tosses the ball back to the pitcher, who snaps it out of the air before giving a prolonged stare in the direction of home plate.

Does this intimidate the umpire and give the pitcher an edge? Think again.

Umpires behind the plate generally fall into three categories: completely objective, friend, or foe. The very best umps are completely objective throughout the entire game. Others start the game unbiased but fall into the latter two categories by game's end.

As the pitcher, you always want the umpire on your side, or at the very least, not against you. That is more important to you than to anyone else on the field. Consequently, follow this simple guideline.

Do not show up the umpire. Do not snap the ball back from the catcher, do not stare in at the umpire, and do not question his calls out loud from the mound. Good umpires understand that a pitcher feels frustration if he thinks he made a good pitch and doesn't get the call. They also recognize that they miss calls from time to time. What they won't tolerate is a player who becomes animated or verbal in protest. It certainly won't work for you, and it could work against you as the game progresses.

This does not mean that an umpire will go out of his way to stick it to you. That is not their mission when they officiate a game. It's the 50/50 calls that will fail to fall in your favor. While umpires strive to be objective at each game, they are human beings underneath that mask. A pitcher who carries himself with maturity and doesn't complain throughout a game will likely get those close calls. The umpire will respect the fact that he's been shown respect. A pitcher who acts out is subject to an ump who takes his antics personally.

There may be a time when you feel the need to ask the umpire a question about his strike zone. The first option is to have your catcher ask him between innings. The catcher is hopefully building a personal rapport with the umpire during the game, so he is the person best suited to be your liaison. A coach may also inquire between innings, provided the coach understands the right way to approach the subject.

The final option is to ask the umpire an open-minded question between innings. Television cameras unfortunately go straight to commercial when an inning is over. If the cameras followed Greg Maddux or Tom Glavine walking from the mound to the dugout after the third out, the picture would occasionally show the pitcher asking the umpire a question about the strike zone. Part of the reason veteran pitchers do it in this fashion is that they know the cameras are not on them, meaning they're not questioning the umpire in front of a national audience watching at home. Umpires appreciate this. If you ever speak to an umpire, check your tone at the door.

The best mind-set is to concentrate on learning the umpire's strike zone. Each guy behind the plate will be slightly different. Adapt to his interpretation of the strike zone (up, down, slightly off the plate, slightly in) and reap the benefits. Fight his judgment and your frustration may adversely affect your performance.

One final note: Umpires *want* to call strikes. There are not too many umpires you'll talk to before a game who say, "I hope this pitcher is wild." They like to call strikes. Appease them by learning their strike zones.

16. Be as good, if not better, pitching from the stretch.

A pitcher is cruising along through the first two innings of a game. The leadoff hitter in the third inning gets on base. Now throwing from the stretch, the pitcher loses a degree of velocity, accuracy, and mound presence.

What happened? He's not as comfortable throwing from the stretch.

Pitchers will sometimes admit that they're more effective throwing from the windup than the stretch. Well, guess what. That had better change, and if you fall into this category, practice throwing two-thirds of your bullpen pitches from the stretch. You should be as good, if not better, pitching from the stretch. This is what separates the men from the boys.

When you think about it, throwing from the stretch is where most games are won and lost. Are you going to strand runners or are you

How you perform from the stretch position is where most games are won and lost.

going to allow them to score? Especially at higher levels of the game, you'll likely spend more time in the stretch position than the windup.

Often the problem pitchers have throwing from the stretch is psychological. They feel less powerful and, as a result, lose confidence and aggressiveness. There is no reason to think arm strength or command is diminished throwing from the stretch position. Major league relievers (including Mariano Rivera) work exclusively from the stretch, even if no runners are on base. Would their employers allow this if the stretch weren't as good a delivery as the windup? No way!

A problem can occur if your attention is divided between the runner and the hitter. If you're 50/50, you're in trouble. Focus completely on the runner or the hitter, not both.

17. Adjust your pace to your success on the mound or lack thereof.

A batter steps up to the plate and the pitcher immediately begins his delivery. He throws a strike, gets the ball back from the catcher, and quickly toes the rubber.

This pitcher is working at a fast pace. He must have a good rhythm going in the game.

Hitters are taught to control the pace of the at-bat. It's preached to them that it's their at-bat and they should dictate the life of their plate appearance. Well, if you're pitching, it's your game. You're holding the ball, and the hitter has to react to what you do. How quickly or slowly you work depends on how you're doing.

When you're pitching well, work fast. It creates an atmosphere in the mind of hitters that you are in control. You're the dominant party. You want it to where it seems as if you're on offense and the hitter is playing defense. It's a psychological advantage. Furthermore, it allows less time for hitters to adjust or settle on a plan for the forthcoming pitch or make mechanical adjustments to their swing. (Fielders love it, too!)

Other times, the game may not be going so well. Whether it be a series of hits, walks, errors, or a combination of the three, the offense is having success and is on a roll. This is a time to slow things down. Breathe, think, adjust, strategize, and so forth. It's not just about slowing yourself down to regain control; it's also about slowing the offense down. During a rally, the offense is alive and kicking and wanting more. Slowing the game down can frustrate the offense and knock some of the wind out of their sails. Go to the rosin bag, step off the rubber, or call the catcher out to talk. Do whatever you need to do to slow things down and calm the storm. This is a simple example of gamesmanship.

Adjusting your pace during the game requires composure. You can't get caught up in the results, but rather pay attention to them and adapt accordingly. Use what's happening in the game to help with what you want to achieve next.

18. The next breaking pitch doesn't have to be better than the last one.

An effective slider is thrown to the batter. He is fooled and swings through the pitch. The pitcher goes back to the well and throws another slider. He leaves it up and it's hammered in the gap for a run-scoring double.

Did the hitter know it was coming? Maybe. But it was the additional effort by the pitcher that caused poor pitch location.

Trying to throw a better breaking ball than the previous one that was successful is a common error pitchers make. After throwing a good one, for whatever reason, they feel the need to throw the next one even better. When attempting to get sharper break on the pitch, the pitcher often gets tense, opens his front side prematurely, and drags his arm. This causes him to get around or under the ball and throw a flat slider that sits. It's the easiest pitch in the world for a hitter to recognize and crush.

Don't make this mistake. If you throw a good one, throw the same pitch to the same spot. Stay relaxed and trust your success. Not too many hitters who have been fooled by a good breaking pitch are hoping to get the same pitch. (Who hits a good breaking pitch, anyway?) A hanger, however, is the ultimate remedy for a batter who was just fooled.

19. Field your position—don't think of yourself as a specialist.

A ball is popped up in the infield. The pitcher calls for it. The first baseman runs in and calls him off only to fail to get to the spot in time, and the ball drops safely.

Why is the pitcher calling for the ball? Because he wants that out just as much as—if not more than—anyone in the field. It's your out— go get it!

There is a general understanding that pitchers should not field balls put into play. They are a last resort and should only glove the ball when absolutely necessary. How this evolved is perplexing and is often the reason behind failed opportunities to secure outs.

The infield pop-up is a perfect example. As the pitcher, don't you want to catch the ball if you can? Then catch it. Since when is a pitcher unable to catch a ball that he's standing under? Position players may not want to hear this, but pitchers are often the best athletes on the field. They're just as sure-handed as anyone, especially when the ball is popped up in their area of the field.

On the list of pop-up priorities, the pitcher is lowest on the totem pole. Each player on the field has priority over the pitcher. The pop-up priority list exists to ensure order on balls in the air where more than one defensive player can catch the ball. But this doesn't mean a pitcher should never catch a pop-up. That's ridiculous.

Once you've completed each pitch, consider yourself a defensive player. At your position, you plug the biggest hole in the field. You cover first on a ground ball to the right side, back up bases, start

Get off the mound and run toward first base on any ground ball hit to the right side of the infield.

double plays, pick off runners, and field bunts and ground balls. Why in the hell can't you catch a pop-up?

Playing good defense from the pitcher's position helps your chances of winning. Just ask Greg Maddux, a four-time Cy Young Award winner with more than 340 victories and 17 Gold Gloves. You can assist on plays directly to secure outs. In addition, the middle infielders can shade more toward the hole if they're confident you will help defend the middle of the field.

Don't consider yourself a specialist. You're a baseball player. Fielding your position with success will contribute to outs and wins.

20. Pick off runners who make mistakes when taking their lead.

A runner with great speed is on first base. After a couple of pitches, he sets out to take his lead. As he looks back to the base to check the length of his lead, the pitcher snaps a throw and picks him off.

Coincidence? Not likely. The pitcher exposed a bad habit in the runner's lead.

Runners make a lot of mistakes that can be exploited when taking leads, especially at the high school level. If you're observant, you can nab the runner and steal an out.

Some common mistakes base runners make leading off first base follow.

- *Crossing the left foot over the right foot.* After the initial step, if the runner uses a crossover step, execute your pick when his left foot lands. He'll have to untangle his feet before getting back.
- *Peeking back at the base.* As the runner gets out to his lead, he shifts his eyes to the base to see how far he is from the bag. Once his eyes leave you, he's vulnerable to a quick pick. Time it right and he's a dead duck.
- *Leaving the ground as he shuffles to a lead.* When the runner gets air under his feet, turn and fire to first. He first has to land before he can change direction and get back to the base.
- *Feet coming together as he gets out to his lead.* As the runner takes steps, he brings his left foot all the way in to his right foot. With his feet together, he has poor balance and can't explode back to first. As his feet come together, fire to first.

Throws need to be crisp and accurate. Footwork and a quick release are essential. Don't "goose" the ball over to first; throw it with some zip. Target the front left corner of the base because that is precisely where the runner is headed.

The base runner crosses his left foot over his right foot (top). The base runner takes his eyes off the pitcher to gauge the size of his lead (bottom). Both mistakes can be exploited by an alert pitcher with a quick move to first.

Practice footwork and your throws regularly. It's the only way to become comfortable and effective. Treat pickoff moves as a significant contributor to your pitching makeup.

21. Always know who is on deck.

With two outs and runners on second and third base in the sixth inning, a left-handed pitcher throws four consecutive balls that just miss the strike zone. The bases are now loaded with a lefty hitter coming to the plate.

Is the pitcher out of gas? Not necessarily. He may have intentionally pitched around the hitter to face a left-handed batter. There is also now a force play at any base.

Always be aware of the hitter standing on deck, especially in crucial situations. It may influence your approach to the hitter up at the plate. This works both ways. With a dangerous hitter on deck, it's in your best interest to challenge the hitter at bat. Whoever would hit before Barry Bonds during his prime years was the huge benefactor of getting good pitches to hit. The last thing a pitcher wanted to do was put someone on base before Bonds, so they attacked the strike zone.

On the flip side, the dangerous hitter may be at the plate with the batter on deck posing less of a threat. In this case, pitch using discretion, not valor. Surround the strike zone with pitches and see if the hitter will get himself out. There are times in a game to put your ego aside and do what is smart. You have to think of the bigger picture rather than that particular battle. Even Tiger Woods lays up from time to time instead of going for the pin because it's the smart thing to do at the time. Tiger wins with incredible ability but also with great discipline and intelligence.

It's important to note that assessing hitters entails more than reading their stat line entering the game. What is most important is what you've learned about them that day. What are their at-bats like during the game? Are they swinging a hot bat, or do they seem to be searching for their swing? Does the hitter get really good swings off you, or does he seem to have trouble figuring you out? Believe it or not, during the 1990 World Series (Cincinatti versus Oakland), a pitcher would have rather faced Mark McGwire than Billy Hatcher. McGwire struggled in the Series (.214, no home runs) and Hatcher (.750, six runs scored) could do no wrong.

Know your opponent at the plate and the hitter that follows.

Pitch Counts: An Inexact Science

Within the past decade, there has been an alarming increase of amateur pitchers who have had "Tommy John" elbow surgery: doctors remove a damaged ligament from the pitching arm and replace it with a ligament from another part of the body. Recovery typically takes 18 to 24 months.

The exact reasons for this undesirable trend are unclear, but high pitch counts have been tabbed as the culprit. Pitch counts have become an obsession in our baseball society, and I feel the attention given to them is misguided. The problem does not lie with the number of pitches thrown as much as it does with young pitchers never giving their arms an *extended period of rest* throughout the year.

Specialization in sports has become another obsession in our culture, and baseball is not innocent. Today, kids have their spring baseball season, summer tournaments, a fall season and tournaments, and then winter training. It is too much! Major league pitchers (who are grown men with bodies that have fully developed) do not throw year-round. They take months off in the off-season. Throwing is an unnatural motion, and kids who pitch need to take a few months off from mound work.

The attention and credibility given to pitch counts lacks common sense. Choosing an arbitrary number for every pitcher that will keep him healthy and fend off injury is ridiculous. To say a certain number is safe and then eclipsing that number is immediately dangerous lacks logic. Is 60 a good number? How about 75? A round number like 100 for high school pitchers? It's understandable that extreme numbers should be avoided, but the idea that a precise number is the answer lacks merit. A smart, observant coach does not need a clicker to determine whether a pitcher has reached his limit. Signs of reduced velocity, diminished command, and fatigued body language are more accurate than an arbitrary number. What's really important is how the pitcher got to that magic number. Was it a breeze or a struggle?

At every level of baseball, each pitcher is different. The physiological makeup of every person varies, and some can handle more

continued

than others. With that, there are several additional factors. Game circumstances matter in terms of whether pitches were thrown in stressful or relaxed situations. Working out of trouble against tough hitters can be more taxing on the body. Also, what types of pitches is he throwing? Is it just fastball-changeup or are there a variety of pitch types and arm angles that can take a greater toll?

Technique (or pitching mechanics) also weighs in. A pitcher who has a polished and fundamentally sound pitching delivery puts less strain on his body. He may be able to handle more pitches than a pitcher who, for example, lands open with his stride foot. Sound pitching mechanics do not make a pitcher invincible to injury or soreness, but they help to increase what a pitcher's body can withstand. In addition, coaches should take the time to develop *more* pitchers. With more pitchers, the workload is spread out, thereby reducing the risk of overload.

If parents and coaches want to give a young pitcher a better chance of not sustaining injury at a young age, they need to give them an extended period of rest during the year. Stop concerning yourself with falling behind or getting ahead. Number of games played, travel competition, and private instruction are overrated. Besides, it's tough to compete when sidelined with an arm injury.

Do you want to know the very best way to help avoid injury to a kid's pitching arm? Stick a soccer ball at his foot, a basketball under his arm, or a fishing pole in his hands. Allow him to play other sports outside of baseball and enjoy recreational activities. It will only improve his athleticism, but more important, it will give him a break from baseball and reinvigorate his hunger and desire for the sport.

5
Hitting

Ask a group of players their favorite thing to do in baseball. Nearly every kid will tell you, "To hit!" There is something about hitting a baseball that brings about pure satisfaction and enjoyment.

A main source of that pleasure stems from how tough it is to hit. "Hitting is the most difficult thing to do in all of sports." That quote came from Ted Williams, who is arguably the greatest hitter who ever played. Hitting presents such a challenge that when you do catch one off the barrel with precise timing, it grips you. If it were easy, it wouldn't captivate such appeal.

You love to hit, but it's a tremendous challenge to experience success regularly. These two points cause internal conflict, and the friction it creates extracts emotions that may be foreign to your personality. You may get angry, fearful, stressed, frustrated, anxious, or even timid. But if you really think about it, those emotions are associated with the result. The act of hitting is still fun, but when the result is not what you want, it causes unrest.

An integral part in using the sixth tool when hitting is learning to enjoy the entire experience of hitting. Enjoy sizing up the pitcher's makeup, observing his patterns, formulating a plan, taking an aggressive swing, and pounding the baseball. You can be serious in your concentration and preparation, but if you relish the challenge of each at-bat, your results will improve. A hitter who genuinely looks forward to hitting and the challenge it offers will have a relaxed body and a clear mind.

It is essential to practice and understand your swing, but there are many additives at your fingertips that sixth-tool players use to supplement their hitting experience. Opening your eyes and ears enables you to recognize the game situation, survey the defense, identify pitch patterns, and make adjustments. "Hitting is a lot more than just picking up a bat and swinging it," said Paul O'Neill, former AL batting champion. "You've got to be observant, evaluate the situation, know the pitcher and his tendencies, and know yourself. If you want to be successful, you have to become a student."

Because it's so challenging, failure at the plate is inevitable. But how do you handle it? Do you allow your emotions to boil over to the point that it adversely affects future at-bats? Or are you able to compartmentalize that disappointment and analyze what needs to be done in your next at-bat to achieve the desired result? It is significant that you learn to deal with failure at higher levels of play because it's going to happen more and more. Pitchers and defenses get better, so stringing together hits gets tougher. When you make an out, look forward not backward. Take a moment to analyze what happened, but leave the failure behind. What is next is what's most important, not something you can't change. That is something the very best competitors understand and apply to hitting.

The majority of sixth-tool thinking occurs before your at-bat. Watching the pitcher, observing your teammates' success or lack thereof, learning the umpire's strike zone, and considering the game situation is information that prepares you for your at-bat. Along with that is an acknowledgment of who you are as a hitter. Are you a left-handed speedster, or are you a 6′2″ power hitter? You've got to be honest with your role in the lineup and tailor your offensive game to your strengths.

Once you dig in the box, however, it's a time to execute. You have a plan in mind, and your body reacts to what your eyes tell it to do or not to. It's that simple. Your mind acts as the general, your eyes as the informant, and your body as the soldier. What the general decides based on what the informant sees, the body does without question or hesitation. If you decide to sit on a breaking pitch, commit to hitting a breaking pitch. Don't think or worry about being wrong. Visualize how hard you'll hit the ball when you're right. You can adapt your plan and make minor mechanical adjustments during the at-bat, but for the most part, your approach is to react to and attack what the pitcher throws.

Finally, practice everything that hitting involves. Practice your situational swings, practice count hitting and zone hitting, practice predicting pitch patterns, and practice controlling your emotions. The only way to get better is to utilize all your resources and develop the primary ingredient to successful hitting—confidence.

Good hitters make adjustments from pitch to pitch. Here, a fastball beats the hitter because he cast his hands out on the swing. Between pitches, he reminds himself to shorten his swing and stay inside the ball.

Tips for the Batter's Box

The following tips are for the advanced hitter's psyche and preparation. Because the pitcher has the ball and decides what he'll throw and where he'll throw it, the hitter needs to call on every resource possible to balance the playing field.

1. Did you make an out, or did he get you out?

After two fastballs on the low outside corner, the pitcher throws a change-up in the same location. The batter hits a hard ground ball to the second baseman, who fields the ball and throws to first for the out.

The hitter failed. Did he really fail, or did the pitcher just do a great job of executing his pitches?

Every time you walk up to the plate, carry the thought that you will hit the ball hard. Think about picking a good pitch and driving the ball for a hit.

The reality is that there are times when you will not hit the ball hard. Swinging through or mishitting balls can be the result of a flawed swing, poor timing, or a lack of plate discipline. There are times, however, when the pitcher makes great pitches. When the pitcher has a plan and executes it to perfection, it's very tough for you to succeed.

This is an important question to ask yourself when jogging back to the dugout: "Did *he* get me out?" If he made great pitches, you have to give the pitcher credit. Don't start questioning yourself and your abilities because he did his job well. That is how some hitting slumps are *created*. A fastball in on the hands, a changeup at the knees, and a slider that breaks just off the plate are quality pitches. You're not supposed to crush them.

There will be times when you get yourself out. When that happens, address the mistake and make the necessary adjustment in your next at-bat. But an out is not necessarily a failure by you. It may simply be an instance of success by a worthy adversary. Don't beat yourself up over it.

2. Your swing should match who you are.

A second baseman is up at the plate. He has a small build but runs very well. With no runners on base and nobody out, he takes his stance in the box. The first pitch he sees is a fastball and he comes unglued. He takes a tremendous swing at a high fastball with a slight uppercut and sends a high fly ball to left-center field. The left fielder drops back, settles under the ball, and squeezes the first out of the inning.

Should he have taken the pitch? Probably, since he was leading off the inning. But more important, his objective should be line drives and hard ground balls, not long balls.

No matter who you are, you must take into account your physical strengths and weaknesses. They act as a blueprint in designing the *type* of hitter that you should be to enjoy optimum success. David Ortiz is not going to swing the bat like Ichiro Suzuki and vice versa. Ortiz is a man of exceptional size and strength. Ichiro has outstanding hand speed and bat control. He also runs very well. Ortiz lets loose with his swing, attempting to generate maximum bat speed and power to hit the ball out front and drive it for distance. Ichiro sees the ball long and keeps his barrel through the hitting zone for a long period of time. He trusts the use of his wrists and hits the ball to all fields to get on base.

Line-drive hitters should see the ball slightly longer and use the entire field.

Ortiz and Suzuki are two great left-handed hitters with two differ-ent swings and approaches at the plate. Each is an American League All-Star and tailors a swing that suits his personal strengths.

When practicing and playing, be honest with who you are. Get really good at the type of hitting that is best suited for you. Tailor your approach to hitting to what makes you the best. It's in your best interest as an offensive player.

3. Your swing should match the count.

A batter has worked the count to 2-0. The pitcher grooves a fastball down the middle, and the hitter brings his hands in and fights off the pitch to the opposite field.

Was this a good 2-0 swing? No. It sounds like more of a 0-2 swing.

The fundamentals of your swing should remain consistent. Pitch location forces you to vary a few things, but generally, your tech-nique remains intact. The timing and aggressiveness of your swing is determined by the count.

Let's, however, take a look at that same 2-0 count. It's likely the pitcher will throw his most accurate pitch (fastball) because he doesn't want to miss and go to 3-0. Taking that into consideration, start everything (stride, load, and then swing) slightly earlier, so you can generate maximum bat-head speed and meet the ball out front. The appearance of a 2-0 swing should be one that is explosive and looks to do damage.

Your two-strike swing should have a different look. While you still maintain bat speed, see the ball a bit longer and stay on the ball longer. This gives you a much better chance of adjusting to a changeup or breaking pitch. Committing early and flashing through the hitting zone is an undisciplined swing with two strikes. It leaves you vulnerable to outside strikes and any pitch that is off-speed.

Your swing for in-between counts, such as 1-1 or 2-1, for exam-ple, should match your plan. Some hitters are count hitters and like to select a certain pitch type to anticipate. When they get that pitch, they go after it. Other hitters are location hitters in these counts. They look for pitches in a certain locations (middle-in, out over the plate, upper half, and lower half). When the pitch is thrown in that location, they go after it.

The approach you take (location or count hitter) may always be the same or it may change throughout the season. What's important is that you have a plan for each count, and avoid thoughts such as, "I don't want to get jammed on a fastball, but look out for the breaking pitch away." Those "in-between" thoughts will get you into trouble.

4. In "pressure" situations, focus on the execution rather than the result.

Down by a run in the final frame, there is a runner on third base with one out. The batter steps up to the plate and the third-base coach yells, "We need a fly ball here."

These are the kinds of words that get hitters into trouble.

The word *pressure* is in quotations because the only pressure felt in baseball is by those who place it on themselves. There are crucial situations in a ballgame that may have a greater impact on its outcome, but this should not be considered pressure. It should be viewed as an opportunity to do something great. Players who look at these situations as a chance to be the hero have a much better chance of actually being the hero.

As mentioned, when walking up to the plate, your thoughts should be that you have an opportunity to do something special. Embrace that potential reward and then shift your focus to the job at hand. Understand what it is you need to do to achieve your goal. Concentrate on pitch selection, a swing thought, a simple reminder, or visualization.

A mistake hitters often make is thinking about the result. They get caught up in the moment. This is where that advice from the coach can cause problems. The body does what the mind tells it to do, and if all you're thinking about is hitting a fly ball, what do you think might happen? Typical mistakes like dropping the rear shoulder, coming out of your swing prematurely, flying open with the front shoulder, and so forth are often the result. These are all mistakes born out of thought. You're trying to help the ball into the air. Focusing on the result can have an adverse affect on your execution.

Take a deep breath and think about what you need to do as a hitter, and if you do things the right way, the result will take care of itself. Stop worrying about what might or might not happen. Engross yourself in one simple thought of execution and all the peripheral elements—the score, the runners on base, the thoughts of your teammates, the coaches, the spectators in the stands—they will all go away. When you think about it, all of that stuff is just window dressing. The pitcher is still the same distance away throwing the same baseball. You're wielding the same bat with the same swing. Don't build up the at-bat to be any different in your mind. Just execute what you've practiced and the results will follow.

Here are some suggested thoughts when you're in this particular situation. These are merely general suggestions. Only you can decide what thoughts work best for you.

PITCH SELECTION

- Get a pitch middle-in
- Get a pitch out over the plate
- Make sure the pitch is thigh-high and above
- Make sure the pitch is below my hands

SWING THOUGHT

- Drive through the ball
- Short and quick

Getting a pitch in *your* hitting zone will bring you the most consistent success in RBI situations.

- Balance from start to finish
- Palm-up, palm-down
- Attack

VISUALIZATION
- Line drive through the middle
- Line drive gap to gap
- Line drive to the opposite field
- Visualize the pitch you're looking for

SIMPLE REMINDER
- Quiet stride
- See the ball long
- Stay inside the ball
- Keep the head down

Whether you use one of these thoughts or employ others, it must remain simple and isolated to one or two. Don't choose five of these thoughts, because too many will cause a traffic jam. Keep it simple and be decisive!

5. When a relief pitcher comes into the game in the middle of an inning, look to jump on a first-pitch fastball.

The opposing team's manager comes out to take the ball from the starting pitcher. He's out of gas and in a jam. A relief pitcher comes in from the bullpen, takes his warm-ups, and toes the rubber.

Should you make him throw a strike? Make it be a good strike and rip it!

Hitters often wrestle with their approach and what they should be thinking at the plate. From time to time, think about what is going on in the mind of the pitcher. It can help map out your plan.

A pitcher coming out of the bullpen wants his appearance to begin on a positive note. A first-pitch strike sends a message to the opposing hitters and to himself. As the movie character Nuke Laloosh echoed in the classic baseball movie *Bull Durham*, "I want to announce my presence with authority!"

Take that knowledge and turn it around on the pitcher. If he wants to pump in a fastball for strike one, greet his fastball with the barrel of the bat. It may not only be the best pitch you see in the at-bat, but think about the psychological impact it has on both teams. The pitcher throws one pitch and it's smoked for a base hit. He immediately loses his edge and wonders if he has good stuff that day. His defense is now concerned about his ability to get outs and the coach is questioning himself for bringing him in. On the flip side, your teammates are given a jolt of confidence. They're looking forward to their at-bat to join the hit parade.

Some hitters may respond to this approach by claiming they need to see a pitch to gauge his velocity, point of release, and movement. Well, that's what you're supposed to be figuring out on deck. Velocity can be seen and timed on deck. Movement is commonly determined by the pitcher's delivery and point of release, both of which can be seen from the on-deck circle. It's not a perfect science, but this is what is meant by taking some risk and being aggressive. If you wait for all the conditions to be perfect, the opportunity may pass.

6. Let the runner steal second base.

With a runner on first base and two outs, the count is 1-0. As the pitcher lifts his leg, the runner breaks for second.

Should you take the pitch, protect the runner by swinging, or think hit-and-run? If you're smart, you'll take the pitch.

With a runner on first base (and less than two strikes), let him steal the base if he goes. It puts him in scoring position and gives you an opportunity to drive him in. Don't worry about giving up a pitch. It's a team play. It's similar to a sacrifice bunt in that you're giving up yourself to advance the runner, except in this case, you're only giving up one pitch.

The same idea applies for a runner on second base trying to steal third with less than two outs. Take the pitch! If he slides in safely, there are 26 ways (according to Gordie Gillespie) that he can score from third base.

Lastly, when the runner goes, stay in the box. Don't duck or step out to make the throw easier on the catcher. Don't interfere, but hold your ground—the rules say that you're entitled to the batter's box.

7. You'll get more fastballs in stolen-base situations.

With a fast runner on first base, the pitcher fires a first-pitch fastball that is pulled foul. The runner holds on the second pitch, which is a fastball that is drilled into the outfield gap.

Why did he throw a second fastball? Possibly because he (or the catcher) is more concerned about the base runner than the hitter.

The attention of the pitcher and catcher is often divided in a stolen-base situation. The pitcher does not want the runner to get into scoring position, and the catcher wants a shot at throwing the runner out if he attempts to steal. Because the fastball gives the catcher his best shot at gunning down the runner, expect to get more fastballs with a speedy runner on base.

This is a great position to be in as the hitter. It's not just about getting fastballs, but you'll often get good fastballs to hit. A pitcher who is concerned about the runner is focusing less on locating his pitches. He wants to get the pitch there quickly. Often he'll rush his delivery, which typically results in pitches being thrown up in the strike zone.

Catchers can get selfish and call for more fastballs, even if it's not the smartest pitch to throw you. A stolen base reflects poorly on them, so they want a chance to throw the runner out. Off-speed pitches thrown down are tough pitches for catchers to receive and throw. Look to capitalize on the heater.

8. Take advantage of predictable pitch patterns.

After a first-pitch fastball for a strike, the pitcher throws an 0-1 breaking ball. The hitter is not fooled and laces a line drive to center field.

Is the batter guess hitting? If it's the pitcher's pattern, it's an educated guess.

Pitchers fall into patterns on the mound. They'll throw certain pitches to start an at-bat, when they get ahead, when they fall behind, and other situations. Watch your teammates' at-bats and what's working for the pitcher. Many times you can expect the same treatment.

Here are a few questions to ask yourself when looking to detect pitch patterns.

- What is he starting hitters off with? Fastball in the strike zone? Out of the strike zone? Breaking ball?
- What pitch does he throw when he gets ahead in the count?
- What pitch does he throw when he gets behind in the count?
- Will he waste a pitch when he's far ahead in the count (0-2, 1-2)?
- What is his "out" pitch?
- Is he trying to set up hitters laterally in the strike zone (inside and outside) or vertically in the strike zone (up and down)?
- When he gives up a hit, does he automatically use a different pitch from the one that was just hit?
- Is there a pitch he always throws in certain game situations (e.g., throws a sinker when he needs a ground ball)?

Many pitchers are predictable during a particular outing because they're lacking success with a certain pitch. A pitcher, for example, may not have command of his slider. If he needs to throw a quality strike with a runner on third base, you can cross that pitch off the list. A simple rule to consider is that pitchers will continue to go with what's working for them and will shy away from what is not working.

Don't be afraid to trust your instinct and look for a pitch, even if it challenges conventional wisdom. You'll be correct more than you think, and remember, you only have to be right once during an at-bat.

9. Cheat if you have to (against velocity).

A pitcher blows a fastball by the hitter for strike one. He comes back with a fastball that is fouled off to the opposite field. The pitcher follows with a third fastball that is driven for a base hit.

Did he lose velocity, or did the hitter gain bat speed? Neither. The hitter cheated.

Cheating at the plate doesn't mean you have to do something against the rules. It means that you start your stride and load slightly earlier in anticipation of a fastball. To catch up to the pitch, you've got to start your swing sooner.

There will be times when you're late on a fastball. The pitcher may have exceptional velocity or perhaps you have a slower bat that day. Whatever the case, you have to do something quick to compete against his fastball. Assume a fastball is being thrown, begin your stride slightly sooner, get your hands back, and make your decision to swing a bit earlier. It's your only chance to get the barrel there in time. Survey the pitch a fraction too long and it will be past you.

Hopefully this will only be a temporary measure that needs to be taken. Cheating leaves you vulnerable to off-speed pitches, so you don't want to make it a habit. If you find yourself having to cheat often, take a look at your load position, stride, or swing path. There may be a mechanical issue that is making you late.

10. Pay attention to the defense before the pitch. They might tell you what pitch is coming.

As the pitcher takes the sign from the catcher in a 1-1 count, the short-stop moves two steps to his right and one step in. The pitcher delivers a breaking ball and the right-handed batter sits back and crushes it to the right-center-field gap.

Why wasn't the batter fooled? The shortstop told him an off-speed pitch was coming.

Attentive defensive players look in for the catcher's sign so they know what pitch is about to be thrown. This helps them establish their positioning and anticipate how the ball will be hit. Some infielders (or outfielders) mistakenly adjust their positioning too early. When this happens the batter can take advantage.

Taking note of this should be done in the dugout or on-deck circle. It's not something to begin searching for when you get up to the plate. Prior to your at-bat, observe the middle infielders and center fielder. They have the best view of the catcher's signs. The most common adjustment is that when an off-speed pitch is called, the fielder will move toward the hitter's pull-side. On fastballs, they'll either stay straight up or shift toward the opposite field.

To accomplish this, two critical factors must be present. First, watch the defensive players for several pitches to verify you're correct. Don't observe a couple of pitches and assume you've picked up a giveaway. Second, make sure they're moving *early*. Defensive players adjust their positioning all the time based on the pitch, but most do it properly. They wait until the pitcher begins his windup and then move. This is not a giveaway. *Do not try* to look around at the

The shortstop is shaded toward second base. This can indicate that an off-speed pitch is being thrown to a left-handed hitter or a fastball is called for a right-handed hitter.

movement of defensive players while the pitcher is in his delivery. It takes your attention away from picking up the pitch, which is more important than anything.

A final point: just because you know what pitch is coming doesn't mean you have to swing at it. If the movement of the second baseman tells you a breaking ball is about to be thrown, you don't have to swing at that pitch. Perhaps the pitch is thrown in an undesirable location, or maybe you want a fastball and will take the breaking pitch, hoping he misses the strike zone. Knowledge of the forthcoming pitch does not always mean you have to take a crack at it. It may simply help you set the table for the following pitch.

11. With two outs, it's a good time for an extra-base hit or stretching a single into a double.

The batter hits a line drive over the second baseman's head for a base hit. He never breaks stride and slides safely into second base.

Pulling this play off entails energy and courage, but it's especially smart if there are two outs in the inning.

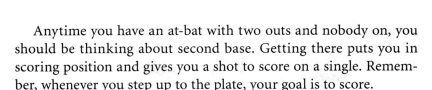

Anytime you have an at-bat with two outs and nobody on, you should be thinking about second base. Getting there puts you in scoring position and gives you a shot to score on a single. Remember, whenever you step up to the plate, your goal is to score.

An extra-base hit is the best-case scenario. Take an approach as you would with a runner on third base and one out. Look for a pitch you can drive from gap to gap. Whether you decide to sit on a fastball and get the barrel out, or sit on a breaking ball and stay back, take a shot at an extra-base hit with an aggressive swing. The only caution is if you do hit a gapper, keep it to a double unless you are 100 percent sure you'll get to third base safely. Don't make the final out at third base.

On a clean single, think double out of the batter's box. (You should always do this, but it's a better time to take a risk with two outs.) When the outfielders have to move laterally to field the ball, you have a greater chance of stretching a single into a double. Balls that force the outfielders toward the foul lines take them away from second base. This is a tougher play for left-handed left fielders and right-handed right fielders. They may take a poor route to the ball or they may be lethargic in their approach. Make your turn around first toward second and decide whether it's a worthwhile risk to stretch it into a double.

Even on base hits that travel directly to the outfielder, anticipate a mistake. Imagine there being a bad hop or miscue in fielding the ball cleanly. Any mishap in execution can provide the window you need to get to second base.

One final suggestion when you're up at the plate with two outs and nobody on. Do not bunt for a base hit unless you are absolutely certain you'll steal second base, preferably early in the count. In most cases, bunting for a base hit in this situation is a no-no unless you are a speedster who will undoubtedly turn a single into a double.

12. With a runner on second base and nobody out, hit a ground ball to the right side.

The score is tied 4–4 in the eighth inning. There is a runner on second base and nobody out. The hitter looks down and gets the bunt sign from the third-base coach.

Why the bunt sign? Because the manager does not have enough confidence that the hitter will be able to advance the runner from second to third with a ground ball to the right side.

This is an example of situational hitting that most players know but don't fully understand. Many fall short in why they need to master it and when this situational swing is in order (or when it's not).

WHY? Your motivation for mastering this situational swing is simple. If the coach doesn't have enough confidence in you to advance the runner by swinging, he'll give you the bunt sign. That is OK, and if you get the sacrifice bunt sign, then you put down a quality bunt. It's a team play. But wouldn't you rather have the opportunity to swing the bat? Hitting the ball to the shortstop's left doesn't guarantee a ground-ball out. You can shoot a ground ball up the middle or in the hole between first and second. You also may hit a line drive over the second baseman's head. If that happens, everybody wins. Give yourself a shot to swing the bat by mastering this situational swing.

Bat control is essential if you want to hit second in the lineup.

WHEN? With a runner on second base and nobody out, your mind immediately goes to moving the runner over. A close game always calls for this situational swing, whether it's early or late. However, it's not a 100 percent guarantee, so communicate with your coach. Perhaps the hitter behind you is struggling and the coach wants you to drive the run in with a base hit. Maybe you're swinging a hot bat and the coach would rather you swing away. Make sure you're on the same page with your coach. Call time-out and talk to the third-base coach if necessary. You don't want to give yourself up to move the runner when your coach wants you to be the guy to drive him in.

Also, there are times when a coach might want you to take one shot at moving the runner over. He may ask you to take one crack at a situational swing. If you foul it off or miss the pitch, swing away. Don't assume anything in this situation because the circumstances at that time may differ from the textbook approach. The important thing is that you've worked on this situational swing to reach a level of competence such that both you and your coach will be confident that you'll get it done.

13. When a pitcher has continued success with the outside part of the plate, take it away from him.

Through his first two at-bats, every pitch the hitter has seen has been on the outside part of the plate. He is 0-for-2 with a weak ground ball to shortstop and a soft fly ball to right field.

What can he do during his third at-bat? Pitchers like to go with what works, so he'll probably be fed more outside pitches. Get up on the plate.

The higher the level of play, the better the pitchers get at locating pitches. It's not just about "stuff." Pitchers are able to command their pitches better and become more knowledgeable of how to get hitters out. Many target the outer half of the plate because they're tougher pitches to hit.

When a pitcher is consistently getting you (and your teammates) out with outside strikes, move up on the plate. This accomplishes two things. First, the pitch on the outside corner will now be more middle-away. Because you've pulled the strike zone in closer to you by moving up on the plate, the outside strike isn't so outside anymore. It's easier to handle. Anything that seems away will definitely be a ball.

The second thing it does is force the pitcher to make a decision. He can continue to throw outside and hope he remains effective, or he may change his approach and try to throw inside. By making the pitcher adjust his approach from what has been successful, you have gained a realistic and psychological advantage. Turn your discomfort into his discomfort.

Tom Glavine has won more than 300 career games living on the outside corner. He doesn't have overpowering stuff, but he changes speeds and his command is exceptional. Former major league outfielder and teammate Dave Gallagher talks about how his approach against Glavine evolved throughout his career.

"Guys would say to beat Glavine, you had to take the ball to the opposite field. But do you know how hard it is to hit a ball hard on the outside corner, especially when he's changing speeds? What I decided to do was get up on the plate. I moved up on the plate because pitching inside is what he liked to do the least. I thought if I forced him to do that, I was taking him away from his strength. Glavine throws inside for effect, not to throw strikes. Also, now that

If the pitcher has continued success throughout a game hitting the outside part of the plate, move up and take it away from him.

I'm up on the plate, the outside corner pitch is like hitting a pitch down the middle.

"When I moved up on the plate I thought I finally had an edge on him. I could see the look on his face when he was out on the rubber that he wasn't happy with where I was standing. The last time I faced him, I went 1-for-2 with a walk. I wouldn't say I owned him, but I think most hitters who've faced him would be happy with that."

14. Listen for or sense a catcher who sets up early.

With a 1-1 count, the catcher calls for an inside fastball. The batter turns on the fastball and rips it to left-center field.

Did the pitcher tip off he was throwing a fastball? Possibly, or the catcher tipped the pitch.

When a catcher calls for an inside or outside strike, he sets up so the middle of his body is centered over that portion of the plate. It provides an inviting target for the pitcher. Good catchers wait as long as possible (until the pitcher is already in motion) before setting up. And they do so quietly.

A catcher who sets up too early can alert you to the called pitch and location. If he's set up inside, look for something hard in on your hands.

However, some catchers are careless. They set up early and you can hear or sense if they are close to you (inside) or away from you (outside). If the sun is at your back, you may be able to see the catcher's shadow.

These are not steadfast rules, but typically when a catcher sets up inside, you're getting a fastball. Stay soft with your stride; get your hips going and your barrel out. When he is set up away, it could either be a fastball or an off-speed pitch, but either way, look to see the ball long.

Some hitters attempt to peek back at the catcher to gauge his location, but beware of trying this. If the catcher notices, he may set up away early and then call for a pitch up and in. Take it as a general rule: if you're trying to steal signs, don't get caught.

15. Consider the pitcher's command and the catcher's ability to block the ball with a runner on third base.

With runners on second and third base, a breaking pitch gets away from the catcher and the runner scores. The runner on second moves up to third base.

Should the hitter still look breaking ball? If he does, he's not paying attention.

Pitchers must have confidence in two things when throwing a breaking ball with a runner on third base. He needs to have confidence that he won't bounce it, and he also has to believe that if he does bounce it, the catcher will block the ball and keep it in front.

Once a breaking ball in the dirt gets away from the catcher, consider it a chink in the armor of that confidence. Whether the pitcher loses faith in himself or the catcher, he does not want it to happen in succession. It's a great opportunity to look for a fastball and capitalize. Even if the pitcher does try throwing a breaking pitch, you can bet it won't be down. Off-speed pitches up in the zone are much easier to recognize (and hit).

16. When taking a pitch, think about showing bunt.

The third-base coach flashes the "take" sign to the hitter. On the ensuing pitch, the batter slides his hands up on the barrel and drops his rear leg back.

Why did he indicate drag bunt? Why not?

Whether you get the "take" sign or want to see a pitch, show bunt from time to time. You can still observe the release point, movement on the pitch, and its velocity. What you can gain is the defensive players might feel they need to now move in. The third baseman may take a few steps forward, which reduces his range and widens your hitting lane. The first baseman may do the same.

Showing bunt may work not only for that at-bat but for future at-bats as well. It plants a seed in the minds of corner infielders. The next time you step up to the plate, someone will inevitably call out, "Heads up, he may bunt." This weighs on the minds of the third and first basemen and encourages them to move up. They fear looking stupid if a bunt is dropped and they've failed to move in.

When taking a pitch, most hitters take their stride and watch the pitch. Why not get something more out of it? Slide your hands up on the bat as you watch it and put the defense on their toes.

17. It's OK to guess breaking ball.

After taking a fastball for strike one, the hitter steps out to gather his thoughts. The next pitch is a breaking ball, and he takes it for a strike in disgust.

Why is he so angry? Because he sensed a breaking ball was coming but decided to look for a fastball.

Just about every hitter would rather hit a fastball than a breaking ball. Pitchers are well aware of this trend. Breaking pitches can be tough to hit. If you know a breaking ball is coming, however, they suddenly become easier to time, track, and strike. In addition, the ones that are thrown out of the strike zone are easier to take.

With this in mind, when you're at bat with less than two strikes and your gut tells you a breaking pitch is coming, look for it! Sit on a breaking pitch. Why wouldn't you? If you're right, you'll have a good rip at a slow pitch with a break you can anticipate. If you're wrong, then you take a fastball and alter your plan in the new count.

Hitters like to stick with looking for what they want, and in many cases it's smart to be stubborn at the plate. The longer you play, how-ever, the more pitchers you will face who have command of their off-speed pitches. They can throw them for strikes consistently. You may never see that fastball you're waiting for, and you'll constantly find yourself hitting behind in the count.

Don't be afraid to look breaking ball if that is what your senses are telling you. Manny Ramirez, Jim Edmonds, Albert Pujols, and many others are examples of hitters who do this with great success. And don't worry about the great breaking ball that you can't hit. You can sit on a Josh Beckett or a Barry Zito breaking ball and be right, but it doesn't mean you'll hit it.

18. Watch the pitcher closely to see if he tips his pitches.

A pitcher toes the rubber and his throwing elbow is relaxed and pointing downward with his hand in the glove. On the following pitch, his elbow is noticeably pointed outward as he takes his grip.

What does it matter where the pitcher's elbow is positioned? It matters because he's tipping his pitches.

To be a pitcher takes an extraordinary amount of focus. Pitchers must be attentive to the game situation, the batter, who is on deck, what pitches are working for them, which are not working, the umpire's strike zone, the slight wrinkle in their delivery, and so forth. Because there are so many variables to consider, they sometimes forget that they are being watched. Pitchers can tip pitches without even realizing it, and by the time they do realize it, it may be too late.

Baseball Etiquette: Bunting in Different Game Situations

Bunting for a base hit is a great weapon to have in your offensive arsenal. When your team has a big lead, however, it's not the time to drop a bunt.

Drag or push bunting with a big lead is considered poor baseball etiquette, or rubbing it in the face of the opponent. It's along the same lines as stealing with a large lead.

In close games, trying to get a rally started, amidst a slump, or if the third baseman is slow-footed and playing deep are all excellent times to try bunting for a base hit. With a big lead, however, keep the bunt on the shelf and swing away.

Take careful watch of a pitcher from the time he takes the sign through his delivery. It may be something very subtle or something obvious. This homework is done from the dugout, not at the plate. Test yourself to make sure you're 100 percent correct. If you're less than 100 percent, he's not tipping. Get up there and hit.

Listed are some things to watch for from the dugout.

- *Pace of his delivery.* Sometimes pitchers will speed up or slow down when throwing a nonfastball pitch. The tempo of the pitcher's delivery can change when he's not throwing a fastball.
- *Digging into his glove.* When you notice a pitcher's glove shaking slightly while he's taking his grip, it's an indication that he's throwing something other than a fastball. He's fidgeting because the way he holds the ball varies from a traditional throwing grip.
- *A relaxed or raised throwing elbow.* Check the pitcher's throwing elbow when his hand rests in the glove. It may be consistent on every pitch, but if it's not, a raised throwing elbow often indicates he's gripping a breaking pitch. When the elbow is relaxed (pointed downward), it's likely a fastball or changeup.
- *The height of the leg raise.* A pitcher may become more tentative with his delivery when throwing an off-speed pitch. He becomes more conscious of command and keeping the pitch down. Because he is not trying to generate maximum velocity, his leg raise may be abbreviated. It will either not go as high, or he will not turn his hips inward as much (showing the batter his back pocket). A more controlled delivery can indicate an off-speed pitch.
- *Taking his grip with the ball outside of his glove in the stretch position.* When a pitcher goes from the stretch, he often turns the ball in his hand to set it up for his grip. With the ball held out of his glove and behind his back, you may notice if he's taking a grip across the seams (fastball) or with the seams slightly off to the side (breaking ball). The runner on first base will have the best view. Perhaps he can pick up the grip and call out a verbal signal. For example, "If I call out your first name—fastball, your last name—breaking ball." Your teammates may be able to observe this as well if they're sitting in the first-base dugout.

- *Wrapping the ball prematurely.* A pitcher who throws a breaking pitch incorrectly often shows his cards before throwing the ball. As his arm swings forward to the release point, his hand will already be turned inward. This is called wrapping the pitch. You'll notice that you'll see less white on the ball because the hand is turned and in view.
- *Facial expression and posture.* When a pitcher looks angry or is standing on the mound like he's a 6′6″ linebacker, a fastball is probably on its way. A more pensive, relaxed look can indicate an off-speed pitch. This is not an absolute, but you may notice pitchers who are more emotional will tip their pitches with expressions and body language.

Discovering a pitcher is tipping his pitches provides more than just knowledge of what he's throwing. It makes you feel as if you have an edge. You feel smarter than him, and that's a true advantage. You approach the plate brimming with confidence.

19. Don't expect the pitcher to make the same bad pitch twice in a row.

A pitcher throws a 1-1 breaking pitch down and away in the dirt. The hitter easily takes the pitch because it didn't even begin in the strike zone.

What should he anticipate on the 2-1 count? Not the same breaking pitch.

When a pitcher throws a bad breaking pitch, don't expect him to come back with another one. A ball thrown wild in the dirt or one that flutters above the strike zone means the pitcher temporarily lost his feel or release point for that particular pitch. It is extremely rare that he would come back with the same pitch. He'll want to throw another pitch that he has greater trust in to reestablish his own confidence.

A high changeup is another example of a bad pitch. When a pitcher misses with his changeup, he wants to miss down. A high change can be sent a long, long way. It's easier for the hitter to recognize (because it's close to his eyes) and is basically reduced to being a slow straight pitch up around the letters. The pitcher will likely be happy he "got away with one" and follow with a different pitch.

Good hitters are courageous and observant and take educated guesses. This is your opportunity to do so. Sit on a fastball after a pitcher misses with an off-speed pitch, especially if he misses badly. He will look to expose your weaknesses at the plate, but insecurity is often a weakness that plagues the pitcher. By sensing his frustration or lack of confidence in a pitch, you can cross it off your list of pitches to consider for that at-bat. In fact, the pitcher may not throw it again until he has a chance to work on it between innings in warm-ups.

With less than two strikes, if the pitcher misses with an off-speed pitch, look for a fastball. You'll be right a lot more often than you'll be wrong.

20. Look for a good fastball to attack after a walk.

A batter just took ball four. The hitter on deck walks up to the plate.

Should he take a pitch and make the pitcher throw a strike, or swing away? It's a good time to be selectively aggressive.

Surrendering a free pass (walk) is a minor failure for a pitcher. He's just allowed a runner to reach first base without earning it. He is also feeling the frustration of teammates and coaches. The last thing he wants to do is walk the next batter.

When you're that next batter, anticipate a good fastball is coming and rip it. Make sure it's a pitch in your hitting zone, but with the pitcher wanting to make sure he gets ahead, the pitch may very well be thrown in the center of the plate.

A thought that enters the mind of a hitter is, "Should I make him throw a strike?" In some circumstances, yes. If the pitcher is having a lot of trouble throwing strikes, it may be best to force him to throw a strike. Also, if it's late in the game and you're behind, you may want to see a strike. Other than that, take advantage. Don't approach your at-bats with a mentality of, "What if this happens?" That's no way to play the game. Take the offensive and seize the opportunity. It may be the best pitch you see in the at-bat.

21. Feel free to stick with your interpretation of the strike zone—until you get to two strikes.

With the count 1-0, the pitcher throws a high fastball. The pitch seems high to the hitter, but he knows the umpire is calling it a strike.

Should he swing? Why would he swing? With zero strikes in the count, the hitter is not forced to swing at a pitch he doesn't like.

Every umpire has his personal interpretation of the strike zone. Part of your responsibility as a competitive hitter is to learn the umpire's strike zone for that day. It's an important component to the game, so you need to be attentive if his strike zone is high, low, tight, or wide.

If you notice the umpire's strike zone does not match your interpretation of balls and strikes, don't worry about it. Stick with what you know until you get to two strikes. Your hitting plan early in the count should be largely based on looking for pitches in your *hitting zone*, not the strike zone. So you and the umpire are judging pitches differently.

If you take a pitch that you feel is outside of the strike zone and it's called a strike, relax. Don't let it adversely affect the rest of your at-bat. Take note of where the pitch was thrown and understand it is part of the umpire's strike zone. You want the umpire to be on your side, and if you complain or show bad body language, it can only work against you.

Once you get to two strikes, you must now shift to the umpire's strike zone. Take into account your observations during the game, both on offense and on defense. Remember, what you think is a ball or strike does not matter. It's his opinion that counts. For that day, he is the almighty judge.

If coaches, parents, or teammates are vocally disagreeing with the umpire, do your best to quiet them down. It's only going to work against you and your team. In utilizing the sixth tool, you're looking for advantages. Insults to the umpire from people seated or standing in the distance at ridiculous angles is a disadvantage.

A few things to note when learning the ump's strike zone: In many cases, short umpires who are set in a lower stance behind the catcher tend to have lower strike zones. Taller umpires in a higher stance have higher strike zones. Their eyes are set at different levels. Pay attention to which of the catcher's shoulders the umpire looks over when calling strikes. He'll call more pitches on that side of the plate strikes because the pitch appears central. Also, umpires who are former position players have tighter strike zones. Umps who were pitchers have bigger strike zones.

And if you have to speak to the umpire or ask a question, try to learn his name. If you don't know his name, call him "Sir." Don't get into the habit of calling him "blue." Would you like to be known as a color?

Where Should Your Eyes Be Looking Throughout the Delivery?

Vision is the most underestimated aspect of hitting. It is so important, yet rarely discussed. Most major league hitters (if not all of them) have above-average to exceptional eyesight. Ted Williams, considered by many as the best hitter who ever lived, had 20/10 vision. He could clearly see from 20 feet what a typical person could see from 10 feet.

Hitters are taught to stride, load their hands, fire their hips, and so on. They are seldom taught where to look and when.

In hitting, there is what's called soft center and hard focus. When the pitcher toes the rubber and begins his delivery, your eyes are in a mode of soft focus. They are very relaxed and set on a general area. The pitcher's face or the front of his jersey is an example of a central location your eyes gaze toward in the early stages of the windup. Once the pitcher's arm swings upward to his release point, your eyes shift to hard focus. This means they're locked in on a specific location, which is the point of release.

Do not shift to hard focus prematurely. Don't try to follow the ball from the time the pitcher breaks his hands from his glove. Your eyes can only stay locked in hard focus on a specific point for a short period of time. Then they tire. If they begin to fatigue as the pitch is released, your eyesight will not be as sharp at the most critical point. Have you ever blinked during a pitch? If you have, you know that's usually when you lose track of the pitch. Blinking will happen if the eyes are set in hard focus for a prolonged period of time.

Your eyes are essential in timing the pitch as well as determining location and pitch type. Simply stated, they are crucial to hitting. Any vision training drills to strengthen or sharpen eyesight are worth their weight in gold. It's tough to hit what you can't see.

Index

Aggressiveness, 4, 5, 30
Arizona Diamondbacks, 60
Arm strength, showing off, 69–70

Baltimore Orioles, 84
Base coaches, 33–34, 35–36, 47, 79
Base hits, cutting the ball off on, 74–77
Base runners, 9
    base coach shouting to, 79
    double "live" sign and, 81–82
    holding of, by pitcher, 100–101
    keeping honest on second, 73–74
    mannerisms indicating stealing, 88–90
    mistakes in lead, 116–18
    pickoff plays and, 43–45, 84–85, 106–7
    on third during a breaking pitch, 140
    throwing behind, 74–77, 87–88, 107
    trailing of, on a sure double, 77
Base stealing. *See* Stealing bases
Baseball etiquette
    of bunting, 142
    shutting down the running game, 51
    with umpire hit by a foul tip, 81
Baserunning, 29–61
    assuming *vs.* anticipating in, 46–47
    avoiding final out at third base, 53
    avoiding freezing on line drive, 38
    breaking pitches in the dirt and, 40–41
    the delayed steal in, 38–40
    drawing a throw to first, 59–60
    drawing throws from outfielders, 60–61
    faking a home steal, 37–38
    length of lead and, 53–55
    look in at catcher's signals, 57–58
    looking *vs.* listening in, 33–34
    one-way leads against left-handers in,
      42–43
    outfielders' positioning and, 35–36

reading the pitcher's "tell," 58–59
risk taking in, 30, 32–33
sacrifice bunt and, 50, 73
scoring a ground ball to infield, 55–56
scoring importance in, 31
shortstop positioning and, 34–35, 85–86
sign stealing from the catcher, 56–57
snap throws and, 50–52, 77–79
stealing home in, 48–49
stealing second in, 42–43, 52–53, 58–59,
    130
stealing third in, 47–48, 50–52
tagging up on foul balls, 41–42
using the slide to advantage in, 45–46
Bases-loaded jam, 105
Baylor University, 24
Beckett, Josh, 142
Belichick, Bill, 19
Body language, 19, 68, 99, 106
Bonds, Barry, 101, 118
Boston Red Sox, 69
Bourn, Michael, 60
Breaking pitches, 86, 101, 126, 140
    bad, 144
    in the dirt, 40–41
    fooling the hitter with, 104, 105
    guessing, 141–42
    repeating successful, 114
    taking advantage of, 40–41
    tip-offs to, 143, 144
Brock, Lou, 15
Bull Durham (film), 129
Bunt situations, 73, 84, 142. *See also* Sacri-
    fice bunt; Showing bunt

Catchers, 9, 30
    double "live" sign from, 81–82
    drawing a snap throw from, 50–52

force plays and, 74
look in at signals from, 57–58
look in at signs and location, 86–87
sensing early set-up in, 139–40
shaking off with fastball counts, 95–96
showing off arm strength, 69–70
sign stealing from, 56–57
signaling for a snap throw, 77–79
stealing third on throwback from,
47–48
Changeups, 86, 103, 126, 144
Character, 1–28
communication with teammates (*see*
Communication)
composure during success, 17
confidence *vs.* cockiness, 26–27
enjoyment of the game, 10–12
the golden rule and, 27–28
hustle, 24–26
need to win, 22–23
playing for memories, 9–10
playing to excel, 15–16
playing with fire, 13–15
practice as play, 16–17
rebounding from failure, 23–24
resolve, 21
risk taking (*see* Risk taking)
self-assessment of, 3
six traits of sixth-tool players, 3–7
stealing signs, 19–21
umpire relations (*see* Umpires, respectful treatment of)
using human nature (*see* Human
nature, taking advantage of)
Clemens, Roger, 103
Coaches. *See* Base coaches
Communication, 18–19, 64–65
Competitiveness, 4
Count hitters, 126–27
Crossover step, 55, 116
Curveballs, 107

D'Amato, Cus, 6
Defense, 63–91
adapting to playing conditions, 79–81
batting practice and, 66–67
cutting off base hits, 74–77
depth as opposite-field outfielder, 90
double "live" sign and, 81–82
dropping foul fly balls, 88
fielding of position, 73–74
at front of base in force plays, 74
with ground ball in shortstop hole,
87–88
guarding lines and over-the-head balls,
82
jab stepping toward second, 79
leaving the bat behind, 83
look in at catcher's signs and location,
86–87

missing targets with low throws, 71–73
pitches signaled by, 133–34
rescuing pitcher with pickoff play,
83–85
reviewing potential plays, 70–71
runner's tip-off to stealing, 88–90
sacrifice bunt and, 73
self-knowledge and, 67
showing off arm strength, 69–70
signaling for a snap throw, 77–79
throwing behind runners, 74–77, 87–88
trailing the runner on a sure double, 77
with two outs and a runner on first,
85–86
wanting and expecting the ball, 67–69
Delayed steal, 38–40, 41
Depth
of opposite-field outfielder, 90
runner's awareness of outfielder's, 35–36
of shortstop play, with two outs, 85–86
DiMaggio, Joe, 9
Division III College World Series, 22
Drag bunting, 140, 142
Durocher, Leo, 5

Edmonds, Jim, 142
Energetic behavior, 4–5
Evans, Dwight, 69

Facial expressions, 19–20, 99, 144
Failure, 2, 21, 23–24, 34, 122, 124. *See also*
Losing; Mistakes
False hustle, 74
Fastballs, 86, 97, 107
after a walk, 145
challenging hitters with, 99
cheating against velocity, 132–33
early set-up for, 140
first-pitch, 109–10, 129–30
shaking off catchers with, 95–96
in stolen-base situations, 131
tip-offs to, 143, 144
Fear, 31, 53–54
Fearlessness, 4, 6
First-and-third situation
drawing outfielder's throws in, 61
faking a home steal in, 37–38
stealing home in, 48–49
First base
aggressive secondary lead on, 77–79
drawing a throw to, 59–60
runner on, with two outs, 85–86
sign stealing from, 56–57
First baseman, 77
First-pitch strikes, 109–10, 129–30
Fly balls, 66, 88
Force plays, 45, 74
Ford, Whitey, 22
Fosse, Ray, 30
Foul balls, 41–42, 88

Foul tip, 81
Francoeur, Jeff, 69

Gallagher, Dave, 34, 74, 138–39
Giambi, Jeremy, 25
Gibson, Bob, 22
Gillespie, Gordie, 29, 130
Glavine, Tom, 103, 111, 138–39
Gmitter, Joe, 51–52
Golden rule, 27–28
Grass, impact on playing, 80
Ground balls, 66, 105, 109
    hit deep in shortstop hole, 87–88
    hitting to right side, 135–37
    scoring to infield from second, 55–56
Guerrero, Vladimir, 14, 69, 101

Hampden-Sydney College, 22
Hard focus, 147
Hatcher, Billy, 118
Hernandez, Keith, 83
Hernandez, Livan, 103
Hickman, Jim, 30
High throws, 72–73
Hill, Aaron, 49
Hitters, 9, 66
    batting stance of, 96, 97
    challenging with fastballs, 99
    count, 126–27
    fooling, 104–5
    location, 126
    pitcher's awareness of, 118
    reading after the swing, 99
    reading before the swing, 96
    reading during the swing, 97–98
Hitting, 121–47
    allowing a second-base steal, 130
    bad pitches and, 144–45
    breaking pitches with runner on third,
        140
    cheating against velocity, 132–33
    defense giveaway of pitch, 133–34
    early set-up by catcher, 139–40
    for execution vs. result, 127–29
    extra-base hits, 134–35
    fastballs following a walk, 145
    fastballs in stolen-base situations, 131
    first-pitch strikes and, 109–10, 129–30
    ground balls to right side, 135–37
    guessing a breaking pitch, 141–42
    interpretation of strike zone, 145–47
    matching to abilities, 124–26
    matching to the count, 126–27
    predictable pitch patterns and, 131–32
    prevention of powerful, 101–3
    responsibility for outs and, 124
    showing bunt and, 73, 140–41
    situational, 136–37
    taking outside plate from pitcher,
        137–39

vision and, 147
    watching for tipped pitches, 142–44
Hitting zone, 146
Home, stealing
    faking, 37–38
    opportunities for, 48–49
"Horns, the" (catcher's sign), 95
Howard, Ryan, 60
Hudson, Orlando, 60
Human nature, taking advantage of, 7–9,
    74, 104

Imaginativeness, 4, 5, 6–7, 30
Infield, scoring a ground ball from second
    to, 55–56
Injuries, avoiding, 119–20

Jab step, 79
Jeter, Derek, 10, 25
Jordan, Michael, 22
Junior College World Series, 19

Kinne, Jeff, 22

LaRussa, Tony, 45, 66
Lau, Charlie, 13–14
Lead runners, 9, 84
Leads
    length of, 53–55
    mannerisms during, 88–90
    mistakes during, 116–18
    one-run, 82
    one-way, 42–43, 59, 60
    primary, 106
    secondary, 60, 77–79, 106
Left-handed hitters, 66
Left-handed left fielders, 135
Left-handed pitchers, 42–43, 48–49, 60
Line drive, avoiding freezing on, 38
"Live" sign, 81–82
Location hitters, 126
Lombardi, Vince, 4
Long, Terrence, 25
Look in. See also Stealing signs
    at catcher's signals from second, 57–58
    at catcher's signs and location, 86–87
    when stealing second, 52–53
Losing, 12
Low throws, 71–73

Maddux, Greg, 94, 111, 116
Martinez, Pedro, 22, 94
Martinez, Tino, 25
Mays, Willie, 5, 45, 64
McGwire, Mark, 118
Mercer County Community College, 19
Micromanagement of players, 33–34
Miller, Ray, 84
Minnesota Twins, 23
Minor leagues, 23

Mistakes, 12–13, 15–16, 27. *See also* Failure
Mitchell, Fred, 22
Moyer, Jamie, 103
Mussina, Mike, 25

New England Patriots, 19
New York Mets, 49, 54
New York Yankees, 25, 49
"No steal" sign, 51

Oakland Athletics, 25
Observant behavior, 4, 7, 18, 30, 33
Off-speed pitches, 96, 97, 99, 101, 105, 131
    bad, 145
    early set-up for, 140
    tip-offs to, 143, 144
    vulnerability to, 133
O'Neill, Paul, 122
Ortiz, David, 125–26
Outfield, cutting the ball off on base hits to, 74–77
Outfield fence, impact on playing, 81
Outfielders
    drawing throws from, 60–61
    look in at catcher's signs and location, 87
    opposite-field, depth of, 90
    runner's awareness of positioning, 35–36
    showing off arm strength, 69
Outs, 103
    assigning responsibility for, 124
    avoiding final at third base, 53
    extra-base hits and, 134–35
    foul fly balls and, 88
    number of per game, 65
    with a runner on first, 85–86

Pettitte, Andy, 49
Philadelphia Phillies, 14, 49, 60
Pickoff plays
    continuing to second following, 43–45
    rescuing pitchers with, 83–85, 106–7
Pitch counts, 103, 119–20
Pitchers, 2, 8, 9, 30–31, 42–43, 48–49
    as closers, 102
    drawing a throw to first from, 59–60
    force plays and, 74
    giving credit for outs to, 124
    jab stepping during delivery by, 79
    left-handed, 42–43, 48–49, 60
    reading "tell" of, 58–59
    relief, 129–30
    rescuing with pickoff plays, 83–85, 106–7
    right-handed, 48
    sacrifice bunt and, 73
    stealing catcher's signs to, 56–57
    taking a one-way lead against, 42–43

taking outside of plate from, 137–39
    tipping of pitches by, 142–44
Pitching, 93–120
    accuracy outside the strike zone, 108–9
    adjusting pace to success in, 113–14
    awareness of hitter on deck, 118
    bad, 144–45
    in a bases-loaded jam, 105
    below bat speed, 103
    challenging hitters with fastballs, 99
    defense signaling of, 133–34
    etiquette of, 110–12
    fastballs following a walk, 145
    fielding of position, 114–16
    first-pitch strikes and, 109–10, 129–30
    fooling the hitter, 104–5
    holding the runner, 100–101
    injury avoidance and, 119–20
    picking off runners, 116–18
    practicing situational, 107–8
    predictable patterns of, 131–32
    to prevent powerful hits, 101–3
    reading hitters, after the swing, 99
    reading hitters, before the swing, 96
    reading hitters, during the swing, 97–98
    repeating breaking pitches, 114
    shaking off catchers with fastballs, 95–96
    from the stretch, 112–13
Pitching mechanics, 120
Pittaro, Sonny, 2, 11
Playing conditions, adapting to, 79–81
Pop-ups, 80, 103, 105, 109, 114–16
Posada, Jorge, 25, 49
Practice
    batting, 66–67
    communication during, 64
    of hitting, 123
    as play, 16–17
    of situational pitching, 107–8
Pujols, Albert, 101, 142

Ramirez, Manny, 10, 101, 142
Reyes, Jose, 32, 54
Rickey, Branch, 46–47, 74
Rider University, 51–52
Right-handed hitters, 66
Right-handed pitchers, 48
Right-handed right fielders, 135
Risk taking, 2, 12–13, 30, 32–33
Rivera, Mariano, 113
Rodriguez, Pudge, 69, 101
Rose, Pete, 29–30
Rowan University, 22

Sacrifice bunt, 19–20, 50, 73, 135–36
Santana, Johan, 103
Schilling, Curt, 103
Schmidt, Mike, 49
Schwartz, Josh, 22

Second base
  awareness of shortstop position from, 34–35
  continuing to after pick off, 43–45
  double "live" sign with runner on, 81–82
  jab stepping toward, 79
  keeping runner honest on, 73–74
  look in at catcher's signals from, 57–58
  scoring a ground ball from, 55–56
  stealing, 42–43, 52–53, 58–59, 130
  throws on force plays at, 74
Shading, 35, 36, 73–74
Shallow outfield depth, 36, 90
Shortstop
  awareness of positioning, 34–35
  conditions indicating deeper play, 85–86
  jab stepping toward second, 79
Showing bunt, 73, 140–41
Sign stealing. *See* Stealing signs
Situational hitting, 136–37
Situational pitching, 107–8
Slide, using to every advantage, 45–46
Smith, Steve, 24
Smoltz, John, 22
Snap throws, 106
  drawing, to steal third, 50–52
  signaling for, during a secondary lead, 77–79
Snapping the ball, 110, 111
Soft center, 147
Specialization, avoiding, 114–16, 119
Spencer, Shane, 25
Stallone, Sylvester, 23
Stealing bases
  delayed, 38–40, 41
  fastballs and, 131
  holding the ball against, 100–101
  home, 48–49
  home (faking), 37–38
  runner's mannerisms indicating, 88–90
  second, 42–43, 52–53, 58–59, 130
  third, 8, 47–48, 50–52
Stealing signs, 19–21, 56–57, 140. *See also* Look in
Strike zone, 21, 110
  pitching accuracy outside of, 108–9
  practicing situational pitches out of, 107
  pulling closer to hitter, 137
  umpire's interpretation of, 18, 111–12, 145–47
Strikeouts, 103, 105, 107

Strikes, 112, 145
  first-pitch, 109–10, 129–30
  strike zone reinterpretation following, 145–47
Suicide squeeze, 20–21
Sun, impact on playing, 80
Sure doubles, 77, 82
Suzuki, Ichiro, 125–26

Tagging
  on foul balls, 41–42
  using the slide to elude, 45–46
"Take" sign, 140–41
Television cameras, impact of, 111
Third base. *See also* First-and-third situation
  avoiding freezing on line drive at, 38
  avoiding making last out at, 53
  runner on with breaking pitch, 140
  stealing, 8, 47–48, 50–52
  throwing behind runners at, 87–88
Thoreau, Henry David, 5
Throwback, stealing third on, 47–48
"Tommy John" elbow surgery, 119–20
Tools, ranking by position, 91
Toronto Blue Jays, 49
Trail runners, 9, 84, 106

Umpires, 23
  hit by foul tip, 81
  interpretation of strike zone, 18, 111–12, 145–47
  respectful treatment of, 17–18, 110–12, 147
Utley, Chase, 14
Victorino, Shane, 69

Vision, 147
Visualization, 129
Voorhees, Randy, 12, 19

Walks
  fastballs following, 145
  unintentional intentional, 102
Welch, Bob, 109
Westrum, Wes, 7
Williams, Ted, 121, 147
Wilson, Glen, 49
Wilson, John, 23
Wind, impact on playing, 80
Winning, 4, 12, 22–23
Woods, Tiger, 22, 118
World Series, 25, 118

Zito, Barry, 142

About the Author

Mark Gola is the author of several acclaimed baseball books, including *The Five-Tool Player*, *The Louisville Slugger Complete Book of Hitting Faults and Fixes*, *Coaching the Little League Fielder*, and *As Koufax Said*. He was an assistant baseball coach at Rider University and Princeton University and as a player at Rider was a northeast region All-American. Currently, he is the director of hitting at Dave Gallagher's All-American Baseball Academy, in Millstone Township, New Jersey. He resides in Robbinsville, New Jersey.